Monograph Book

In Vitro STUDIES ON *Centella asiatica* (L.) URBAN, AN AYURVEDIC MEDICINAL HERB

Editors
S. Alagumanian
M. V. Rao
S. Sobana

Published by

JPS Scientific Publications
India

Published by

JPS Scientific Publications, Tamil Nadu, India.
E.mail: jpsscientificpublications@gmail.com
Website: www.jpsscientificpublications.com

Published in India.

International Standard Book Number (ISBN): 978-81-946500-7-2

ISBN: 978-81-946500-7-2

ABOUT THE EDITOR - Dr. S. Alagumanian

Dr. S. Alagumanian, M.Sc., Ph.D., PDF, FBSS Assistant Professor (Head), PG and Research Department of Botany, H.H The Rajah's College (Autonomous), Pudukkottai, Tamil Nadu, India. He is doing research in Nano-Biotechnology, Plant Tissue culture. He Guidance render of Ph.D ongoing 3 students in Nano-Biotechnology and Pharmacognosy and completed 8 students in the field of Biotechnology. He has organized 3 International and 5 National conferences and also published around 15 papers in well reputated Journals. He has visited 7 countries and awarded 3 major and 5 minor projects. He has presented his Research work around 80 National conference and 20 International conferences. Research interested with Nano particle and Drug Delivery, Bio-molecule Diagnosis and Reviewer of Elsevier Journal.

ABOUT THE EDITOR - Dr. S. Sobana

Dr. S. Sobana M.Sc, M.Phil, B.ed, Ph.D is currently working as Lecturer in the Department of Physics, H.H. The Rajah's College (A), Pudukkottai. She did her Ph.D in Nano-Physics awarded at Periyar EVR college (Auto), Department of Physics, Triuchirappalli, TN, India., She has been involved with teaching and Research Interest in the area of Nano-physics and Nanoscience. She has presented her Research work in many National and International Conferences. She has published 03 Research papers in well reputated Journals with high Impact factors. She has been Qualified Tamilnadu State Eligibility Test for Assistant professor (TNSET) in the year of 2017.

Contents

Chapter Number	Chapter Title	Page Number
1	Introduction	1
2	Review of Literature	5
3	Materials and Methods	14
4	Results	25
5	Discussion	69
6	Summary	88
7	References	93

1. INTRODUCTION

Distribution

Centella asiatica (L.) Urban, a medicinal herb, is a member of the family Apiaceae. The genus consists of 33 species, and distributed in tropical and sub tropical regions such as India, China, Sri Lanka, Indonesia, Australia and Southern and Central Africa (Chopra *et al.,* 1984). In English: Indian penny wort; Hindi: Brahmamanduki; Tamil: Vallarai; Telugu: Saraswataku; Malayalam: Muttil; Kannadam: Vondelaga; Sanskrit: Mandukaparni.

It is a prostrate, faintly aromatic, stoloniferous perennial herb, grows up to 2 m long, commonly found as a weed in crop fields and other waste places throughout India upto an altitude of 2,000 ft. The stem is glabrous, pink and striated, rooting is at the nodes; leaves are fleshy, orbicular-reniform, crenate-dentate, base cordate and often lobed, long petioled, smooth on the upper surface and sparsely hairy on the lower; flowers are red, pink or white in fascicled umbels and fruits are oblong, dull brown, laterally compressed, pericarp hard and thickened woody, white (Anonymous, 1988). It has a chromosome number of 2n = 18 (Bell and Constance, 1960).

Medicinal importance

C. asiatica has been utilized as a medicine in India since the prehistoric times (Castiglioni, 1958). Fresh extract of the plant has been used for medicinal purposes by the people of Java and other Islands for the healing of wounds (Suguna *et al.,* 1996; Srivastava *et al.*, 1997; Rao *et al.,* 1996) and relief for leprosy (Boitean *et al.*, 1949). The plant extract has been incorporated into the Indian pharmacopoeia (Gupta *et al.*, 1999) and recommended not only for wound healing but also specially for the treatment of skin lesions and diseases such as lupes, exzema, leprosy, psoriasis (Lucia *et al.*, 1997) and to improve the learning memory (Nalini *et al.*, 1992; Asok and Vaidya 1997; Anbuganapathi, 1995; Rao Mohandas *et al.*, 1999; Bharadwaj and Srivastava 1995; Karnick, 1989; Kumar *et al.*, 2000). In pharmacological and clinical trials it has been found to improve the power of concentration and general ability and behavior of mentally retarded children (Rajagopalan, 1995; Handa, 1994; Agarwal *et al.*, 1999; Singh, 2000).

Some significant activities reported on the plant are anti-mutagenic effect (Edwin *et al.*, 2000), antistress (Chatterjee *et al.*, 1992), antibacterial, antifungal (Gurip- fabin *et al.*, 1997; Suchitra *et al.*, 1999), antifeedant (Anonymous, 1988), anticancer (Babu and Pedikkala, 1993; Mathew and Unithan, 1992), antifilarial (Srivastava *et al.*, 1997; Sarkar *et al.,* 1998; Chakraborty *et al.,* 1996), anti tuberculosis (Srivastava *et al.*, 1997) and antigiardial (Abbas *et al.,* 1999). The aqueous suspension of this plant was a significant improvement of immunostimulant activity in rats (Patil *et al.*, 1998; Singh, 2000). The plant contains triterpenes glycosides, thankuniside and isothankuniside and small amount of resin, tannin, saponin, and anthraquinone (Ghani, 1998). The leaf juice is useful in catarrh and other eye troubles. The whole plant is tonic, digestive and diuretic. The plant is used in combating dysentery and convulsive disorders (Hossain *et al.*, 2000). The plant also contains asiaticoside, sapogenins, the bitter principle vellarin, the alkaloid hydrocotylin, the glycosides and the centellosides (Duke and Ayensu, 1985; Glasby, 1991).

The hydro-alcoholic extract of *C. asiatica* showed anxiolytic/sedative effect in the elevated plus maze, potentiation of the hypnotic effect of pentobarbitone and anticonvulsant activity against pentylenetetrazol- induced convulsion (Lucia *et al.*, 1997). It was also effective in controlling the somatic and psychic anxiety (Kuppurajan, 1995). The plant is used as an antidote to cholera. A cold poultice of the fresh herb is used as an external application in rheumatism, elephantiasis and hydrocele. For treating leprosy and other skin diseases it is given as an ointment or dusting powder. Compound proprietary preparations of the plant have been patented for cosmetic use in France. Internally it has been valued as a tonic and is used in bronchitis, asthma, gastric, catarrh, leucorrhoea, kidney troubles, urethritis and dropsy. A decoction of very young shoots is given for hemorrhoids (Chopra, 1958; Chopra *et al.*, 1935; Anonymous, 1958; Burkill, 1909).

The plant showed good therapeutic effects on peptic ulcers. It, one of the components of the drug 'Geriforte', is used for senile pruritus. A paste of the plant is applied to boils and tumors. The whole plant mixed with *Drymaria cordata* Willd and *Oxalis corniculata* L. is boiled and taken to cure dysentery. In large doses of the plant acts as narcotic, producing cephalagia, vertigo and sometimes coma. The plant is considered as aphrodisiac and used in venereal diseases (Anonymous, 1988). It has been found to have considerable sedative action (Ramaswamy *et al.*, 1970; Agarwal, 1981). The drug showed significant improvement in cases of anxiety neurosis (Singh *et al.*, 1981) and peptic ulcer (Chao *et al.*, 1981). It has also been found to cure general debility (Rao *et al.*, 1973) and improve the faculty of memory-retarded children (Sharma *et al.*, 1985).

Madecassol an extract of the plant containing madecassic acid, asiatic acid and asiaticoside accelerates cicatrisation and grafting of wounds. Madecasoside and madecassic acid also show anti-inflammatory activity (Anonymous, 1958; Kritikar and Basu, 1935). A syrup of the leaves with ginger and black pepper is taken for cough. Leaf juice with palm jaggery is given to women as a tonic after delivery. The leaf juice is rubbed on the fore head to cure severe headache. Mixed with bath water, it is used in eczema. The leaf extract is used in the preparation of medicated oil for borne fracture (Anonymous, 1954).

Moreover, *C.asiatica* is an ideal species to restore the degraded land. Its multiple uses, demand in market and high price provide an opportunity to enhance the agriculture productivity and opened new vistas to improve the productivity of the species.

Conventional methods of propagation

Seed, stolons and stem cutting are the conventional propagation (Anonymous, 1951; Rao, 1965). Propagation through seed is unreliable due to poor germination and death of young seedlings under natural conditions (Anonymous, 1988). Because the seeds are often found on the ground, loss due to the rodents is considerable. Moreover, poor seed viability, low rate of germination and increasing human and livestock population have already affected the status of wild plants, particularly of those used in herbal medicine.

Need to incorporate non-conventional methods

Medicinal plants are of great interest to the researchers in the field of biotechnology as most of the drug industries depend, in part, or plants for the production of pharmaceutical compounds (Chand *et al.*, 1997). With an increasing worldwide demand for plant derived medicines and formulations, there has been a concomitant increase in the demand for raw material (Parnham, 1996).

Pharmaceutical companies largely depend upon material produced from naturally occurring stands, which are being depleted rapidly raising concern about possible extinction of the species and providing justification for the development of *in vitro* propagation techniques for these plants (Patra *et al*., 1998).

Natural stands of *C.asiatica* are fast disappearing and threatened with extinction due to discriminative collection and over exploitation for medicinal and commercial purposes and to meet the requirement of the pharmaceutical industry. *Ex situ* conservation can only help in sustainable use of biological resource with net species improvement.

In view of this, there is an urgent need to apply innovative approaches of plant biotechnology that offer a rich scope for creation, conservation, utilization and characterization of genetic variability for plant improvement and rapid cloning of elite germplasm. Though the multiple uses of the *C. asiatica* have been extensively studied and its importance is known worldwide, the knowledge is less adequate in *in vitro* studies. Plant tissue culture is a useful tool for the conservation and rapid propagation of rare and endangered medicinal plants (Saxena *et al*., 1997; Castillo and Jordan, 1997; Sanyal *et al*., 1998). Asiaticoside (a complex mixture that is very difficult to synthesize artificially) can be extracted from micropropagated plants under organized cultivation or through callus or suspension culture. From the pharmaceutical point of view, the most useful is the propagation from excised meristems (direct) since by this method identical plants with desired traits are obtained.

In light of this, the present study was carried out with the following objectives:

1. To propagate *C.asiatica* using micro propagation technique,
2. To study the various factors affecting organogenesis,
3. To study the various factors affecting somatic embryogenesis and
4. To standardize the preliminary phytochemical studies.

2. REVIEW OF LITERATURE

The ability of individual cells to develop into whole plants, known as totipotency has formed the basis for regeneration and propagation of selected genotypes through tissue culture. The totipotency theory was first proposed and clearly formulated by the German botanist Haberlandt in 1902. Unfortunately, his attempts to regenerate plants from palisade mesophyll cells of *Daucus carota* in a simple hormone free medium were not successful. The major break through in tissue culture came after the discovery of auxins, cytokinins and coconut milk in promoting rapid cell divisions and growth of plants (van Overbeek, 1942; Gautheret, 1947; Caplin & Steward, 1948; Miller *et al.*, 1961). It was demonstrated that they stimulated cell division. Addition of cytokinins and auxins to the culture media rendered plants to form callus tissue, roots and/or shoots *de novo*.

Micropropagation

Murashige (1974) and Morel (1960, 1975) were the pioneers in applying meristem culture for rapid clonal propagation, virus elimination and germplasm storage. Various scientists attempted to culture cells and root tips *in vitro* and were unsuccessful (Street, 1977; Gautheret, 1985). Micropropagation offers the potential to produce thousands or even millions of plants per annum. In many cases, the rapid increase serves as a valuable initial boost for the establishment of a large population prior to multiplication by conventional means (Damianl *et al.*, 1983). Micropropagation also provides a means of germplasm storage for maintenance of disease free stock (Wilkins and Dodds, 1983; Withers, 1989). The potential developments, achievements and various problems concerning microporpagation has been reviewed (Murashige, 1974; Hussey, 1986) and described in recent books (Bajaj, 1986, 1988; Thorpe *et al.*, 1991; George, 1993; Narayanaswamy, 1994; Pareek and Swarnkar, 1997). Multiple shoot formation from *Aristolochia indica in vivo* explants such as shoot tip and axillary nodes on medium containing BAP (0.5-2.0 mg/l) in combination with NAA (0.5 mg/l) has been reported by Manjula *et al.* (1997). Auxin supplemented to MS media in shoot apex culture is usually IAA, NAA and IBA which result in multiple shoot production in herbaceous plants (Dodds and Roberts, 1990; Manjula *et al*., 1997; Shrivastava and Rajani, 1999; Vandemoortele *et al*., 1996; Pattnaik and Chand, 1996; Sudha and Seeni, 1994 and 1996). The principal application of micropropagation is the mass propagation of superior plants. In many instances, conventional propagation is a slow process during which disease and pest problems can limit production (Smith and Drew, 1990). In *Gloriosa superba*, micropropagation was achieved by using shoot tip and corm buds (Siva Kumar and Krishnamurthy, 2000). Rapid clonal multiplications of *Angelonia salicariefolla* from nodal explants were reported by Datta and Datta (1984). Axillary node explants have been found to regenerate multiple shoot s in a few medicinal plants such as *Coriandrum sativum* (Kataeva and Popowich, 1993), *Cleistanthus collinus* (Quraishi and Mishra, 1998), *Adhatoda beddomei* (Sudha and Seeni, 1994), *Rauwolfia micrantha* (Sudha and Seeni, 1996), *Ocimum americanum* and *O. sanctum* (Pattnaik and Chand, 1996). Multiple shoot formation and shoot tip and nodal explants were also observed on *Ocimum sanctum* (Begum et al., 2000). Muthukumar *et al*. (2000) have used multiple shoot formation from hypocotyls as an assay system to identify the regeneration potential of different genotypes of *Datura metel*. Lakshmanan *et al*. (1997) reported multiple shoot formation from shoot tip and axillary nodes of *Ixora coccinea* cultured on woody plant medium supplemented with BAP (2.5 mg/l).

Multiple shoot formation from cotyledonary node explants were also observed in litchi (Das *et al*., 1999), shoot buds and axillary nodal explants in mulberries (Pattnaik and Chand, 1997), shoot base in *Safed musli* (Purohit *et al*., 1994), seedling and mature culturing nodes in *Gymnema elegans* (Komalavalli and Rao, 1997). A MS medium, supplemented with 1.0 mg/l BAP and 0.3 mg/l GA_3, was used to induce multiple shoot formation from nodal segments *Tridax procumbens* (Sahoo and Chand, 1998a).

IAA in *Tridax procumbens* (Sahoo and Chand, 1998a), IBA along with IAA in *Vitex negundo* (Sahoo and Chand, 1998b) and IBA alone induced roots in *Gymnema sylvestre* (Komalavalli and Rao, 2000). For rooting of *in vitro* raised shoots, half strength MS basal medium supplemented with IBA (1.0 mg/l) and IAA (0.5 mg/l) was used in *Elaeocarpus robustus* (Roy et al., 1998).

In recent years, there has been an increased interest in *in vitro* culture techniques which offer a viable tool for mass multiplication and germplasm conservation of rare, endangered aromatic and medicinal plants (Arora and Bhojwani, 1989; Sharma *et al.*, 1991; Sudha and Seeni, 1994). The various aspects of micropropagation in different Apiaceae members are presented in Table 1. The general problem met in mass propagation of Apiaceae members is the production of few shoots with the intervention of callus. Hence, factors limiting the efficient micropropagation need to be studied.

Organogenesis

Organogenesis is the formation or development of an organ or even whole plant by the experimental manipulation of plant cell or tissue in *in vitro* under controlled and aseptic conditions (Hicks, 1980). In most cases, organ production under *in vitro* culture, the factors affecting and the nature of developmental events favoring the organ determination were clearly understood (Trolinder and Shang, 1991; Litz and Gray, 1992). Therefore, information from such basic studies are essential for programming applied aspects of research. Recent research works revealed different pattern of organogenesis (Murashige, 1974; Torrey, 1977; Winton, 1978). The process of organogenesis includes callus formation leading to organ differentiation. Regeneration of plantlets from explants without callus formation was demonstrated by Bajaj and Dhanju (1979). Organogenesis from callus cultures was reported by Gosal and Bajaj (1979) and Singh *et al.* (1982).

An efficient plant regeneration system is a pre-requisite for development of disease resistant plants through *in vitro* culture technology with or without using the techniques of genetic engineering (Mc Nicol and Graham, 1990; Litz and Gray, 1992; Aminuddin and Singh, 1995; Yadav *et al.*, 1996; Buyukalaca and Mavituna, 1996). Tissue culture offers new avenues in the application of genetic engineering techniques and the exploration of genetic variants, when organogenesis is attained (Mendoza and Futsuhara, 1990). Ozgen *et al.* (1998) reported regeneration of plantlets from different explants and callus culture of *Onobrychis viciifolia.* Shoots and viable plants were obtained from green nodular callus derived various explants of *Azadiracta indica* (Abubacker and Alagumanian, 1999).

Skoog and Miller (1957) reported that organogenesis in tissue culture was governed by the proportion of auxin and cytokinin in the medium and can not be demonstrated universally due to the explant sensitivity or the original context of endogenous growth regulators. In *Plumbago zeylanica*, plant regeneration was achieved from leaf and stem explants by Rout *et al.* (1999) on MS basal medium supplemented with BAP (4.44 µM), IAA (1.42 µM) and 3% sucrose. Prem and Xu (1999) studied shoot bud regeneration from primary callus of root and leaf on MS medium supplemented with BAP (3.0 mg/l), 5% coconut milk and 60 g/l of sucrose. Shoot bud regeneration from immature leaflets of *Arachis hypogaea* was reported by Bajaj *et al.* (1981), Narasimhulu and Reddy (1983), Atreya *et al.* (1984), Seitz *et al.* (1989), Mckently *et al.* (1991), Cheng *et al.* (1992). Abubacker and Murugesan (1999) obtained plant regeneration from the various explants of sweet sorghum. Influence of growth regulators on plant regeneration from epicotyls and hypocotyls cultures of groundnut (*Arachis hypogaea*) were reported by Venkatachalam *et al.* (1998). In *Hybanthus enneaspermus*, callus induction and plant regeneration were observed (Prakash *et al.*, 1999) from seed explant cultured on MS medium with BAP (1.0 mg/l) and NAA (0.5 mg/l). Regenerated shoots were rooted on half strength MS medium containing IBA (1.0 mg/l). The regenerated shoots were successfully transferred to pots for further evaluation. Plant regeneration from axillary node has been reported in *Gymnema sylvestre* (Komalavalli and Rao, 2000). Maximum shoot bud differentiation (100%) occurred in leaf explants were placed with their adaxial surface and stem explants were placed horizontally in the MS medium containing BAP or KN (2.0 µM) and 0.2% gelrite in *Bacapa monnieri* (Srivastava and Rajani, 1999). Gupta *et al.* (1997) reported plant regeneration from cotyledonary nodes along with shoot apex of cotton on modified MS medium containing BAP (22.2 µM). Efficient *in vitro* shoot regeneration response in leaf explants of *Neoregelia cruenta* were reported (Carneiro *et al.*, 1999). A system using cotyledonary node and shoot tip as explants and BAP (1.5 mg/l), Ads (1.0 mg/l), 2ip (0.5 mg/l) and GA_3 (0.5 mg/l) containing medium was developed for *in vitro* multiple shoot proliferation of *Macrotyloma uniflorum* (Mohamed *et al.*, 1999). Plant regeneration from cotyledonary explants derived callus in *Corchorus capsularis* (Jute) was obtained on a medium containing NAA (2.7 µM) and BAP (4.4 µM) (Saha *et al.*, 1999). Cotyledon and hypocotyl explants of *Aegle mormelos* were cultured on MS basal medium supplemented with different auxins in factorial combination with cytokinins (Arumugam *et al.*, 1997). Plant regeneration from leaf and shoot explants were reported in *Sempervirum tectorum* by Dobos *et al.* (1994). Arockiasamy *et al.* (2001) reported high regeneration nature of plantlets from different explants and callus culture of *Paspalum serbiculatum*. However, understanding of these stimuli and conditions was fragmentary. Studies investigating the organogenic potential of Apiaceae members are presented in Table 2. The little success in organogenesis has reported mainly because of their recalcitrant nature.

Somatic embryogenesis

The development of embryos from somatic cells of any explant through embryological stages stimulating zygotic embryos is called somatic embryos or embryoids and this process is called somatic embryogenesis. This was first observed in carrot (*Daucus carota*) root tissues cultured *in vitro* by Reinert (1958) and Steward (1958a and b) and from a woody angiosperm *Santalum album* by Rao (1965). Differentiation and development of somatic embryos required lowering the concentration or complete elimination of auxin used in the induction medium.

In Apiaceae, generally somatic embryogenesis and plantlet regeneration were achieved in a three step process viz., (i) callus induction (ii) somatic embryo initiation and development and (iii) germination of matured somatic embryos (Wakhlu and Sharma, 1998). The most advanced results have been obtained in *Bacopa monnierie* shoot regeneration via somatic embryogenesis (Tiwari *et al.*, 1998). Enhanced vigor of dry somatic embryos of *Medicago sativa* with increased sucrose was reported (Anandarajah and McKergie, 1990). Somatic embryos and plant regeneration from shoot base cultures of seedlings of garden leck (*Allium pottum*) were reported (Hong and Debergh, 1995). Yu *et al.* (1990) developed somatic embryos from cell suspensions derived from young petioles of *Medicago sativa*. The frequency and the rate of somatic embryogenesis in the suspension cultures were investigated. Heat treatment was optimal between 30 and 33°c for shoot survival and plant regeneration from day embryos (Anandarajah *et al.*, 1991)

A protocol for a high frequency somatic embryogenesis was developed for biotechnological manipulations of hybrid popur in which embryogenic callus was derived from non embryogeneic explants (Micher and Bauer, 1991). Effect of organic acid pretreatment on the regeneration and development of whole plants from callus cultures of a *Medicago sativa* was reported (Nichol *et al.*, 1991). Low O_2 or high CO_2 were shown to stimulate both somatic and zygotic embryogenesis (Norstog and Klein, 1972; Johannson and Eriksson, 1984) and to limit precocious germination (Carman, 1989). The growth inhibitors like abscisic acid (ABA) and 2,3,5 - tri indo benzoic acid (TIBA) at low concentrations favored the normal development of somatic embryos (Ammirato, 1972).

Enhancement and repression of somatic embryogenesis in cell cultures of carrot by cold pretreatment of stock plants were reported (Krul, 1993). The embryos developed into plantlets on MS medium supplemented with IBA (15.0 μM) and BAP (2.2 μM). Barna and Wakhlu (1993) reported somatic embryogenesis and plant regeneration from immature leaflet callus of chickpea. They found that numerous globular embryos differentiated into mature embryos upon removal of 2,4-D. A new basal medium for embryo development *in vitro* was formulated on the basis of the mineral composition of embryos and sucrose, fructose and glucose were compared as carbohydrate sources (Pellegrineschi *et al.*, 1997). Plant regeneration via somatic embryogenesis in pigeon pea (*Cajanus cajan*) has been reported (Srcenirasu *et al.*, 1998). Somatic embryogenesis in cell suspension cultures of pigeon pea (*Cajanus cajan*) has been reported (Ramesh and Ganapathi, 1999). Somatic embryogenesis from leaf and leaf-derived callus was observed in *Tylophora indica* (Manjula *et al.*, 2000). Somatic embryogenesis in *Vigna radiata* was reported (Girija *et al.*, 2000). The various aspects of somatic embryogenesis in different Apiaceae members are presented in Table 3.

Phytochemical study

A large number of medicinal plants are exploited from the natural flora for commercial production of drugs (Paul et al., 1992). The search for new drugs from plants of medicinal value is the most rapid and less expensive for determining the utility of plant species (Cox *et al.*, 1989). Fakin and Sewraj (1990) screened some medicinal plants occurring in Mauritius. Abu-Said *et al.* (1995) investigated some Malaysian plants for secondary metabolites. Tanira *et al.* (1994) carried out phytochemical screening of some medicinal plants of United Arab Emirates.

Tripathi *et al.* (1996) presented a review on the uses of piper species and their secondary metabolites. Anubha (1996) carried out phytochemical evolution of twenty-two multipurpose tree species for their economically important active chemical constituents. Coe (1996) screened 229 plants species used for medicinal purpose to assess the chemical nature of bioactive compounds. Mandi and Sharma (1994) investigated 1500 species of Zingiberaceae for their chemical constituents. Parvati (1997) screened some potential aquatic plants for secondary metabolites.

Earlier Farnsworth (1966); Bhakuni *et al.* (1969); Das and Bhattacharjee (1970); Joshi *et al.* (1974); Odebiyi and Sofowora (1978); Gupta (1980a and b); Saxena and Vyas (1981); Mossa *et al.* (1983); Chhabra *et al.* (1984); Nautiyal and Semwal (1984); Nandi *et al.* (1985); Rao *et al.* (1985); Sudarsanam (1987); Sabins and Danieal (1990) and Reddy (1995) and have undertaken preliminary phytochemical studies on certain medicinal plants.

The phytochemical study regarding *C.asiatica* was carried out by number of people. The samples of Indian variety of *C.asiatica* were collected from different places showed in the presence of glycoside. This crystalline glycoside was isolated and was named asiaticoside (Bontems, 1942). The chemical nature of the active principle of *C.asiatica* is triterpenoid compound (Asakawa, 1982). Similarly the Celonese and Indian varieties were examined and it had been reported that the triterpenes and asiaticoside of both the varieties were not same. This was mainly due to the different geographical conditions (Bhattacharya and Lythgoc, 1967).

Improved yield of ajmalicine and serpentine in *Catharanthus roseus* cell cultures were noted due to precursor feeding (Hay *et al.*, 1988) and hormonal changes (Zenk, 1977). Plant cell culture and sign of development is reviewed by Dougall (1980); Withers (1978) and Withers and Street (1977). Kokate (1995) reported that light and temperature shift could increase the alkaloid production of *C. roseus* cultures. Kokate

(1995) and Tabata *et al.* (1978) demonstrated that callus cultures of *Cassia tora* could produce more than 10 times of anthraquinone derivatives (6%). Zenk *et al.* (1977) reported the production of anthraquinone glycosides increased two folds by the supply of precursor O-succinyl benzoic acid in cell cultures of *Morinda citrifolia.*

The preliminary phytochemical studies showed, leaf and callus materials containing more or less similar secondary compounds. *Aegle marmelos* seed as a new protein source was identified by Banerjee *et al.* (1982) through pharmacognostic studies. Roy *et al.* (1975) have done graded hydrolytic studies on bael gum. Goel *et al.* (1997) reported isolation of compounds luvangetin and pyranocoumarin from the seeds of *Aegle marmelos.* A wide range of phytochemicals have been detected in plant cell cultures (Kokate, 1995 and Fowler, 1983) and this has led to the possibility of some of these compounds being produced on commercial scale. Biotransformation of steroids and cardiac glycosides by plant cell cultures have been studied extensively and reviewed by Reinhard (1974), Alfermann *et al.* (1977), Furuya (1978) and Stohs (1977).

Govind *et al.* (1992) reported that isolated the quaternary alkaloids in stems of *Magnolia acuminata.* A wide range of phytochemicals had been detected in plant cell cultures (Fowler, 1983). Biosynthesis of flavones and flavonols had been extensively studied by Hahlbrock (1977). Davies (1972) reported tannins; Williams and Goodwin (1965) reported xanthin, steroids and terpenoids in rose tissue culture studies.

Generally, medicinally important plant products are secondary metabolites that are synthesized at variable periods of growth and developments. By definition these metabolites are either biologically or pharmacologically active compounds. As they are produced in low amounts substantial quantity of raw plant material is required to extract only a few grams of useful products. Therefore novel methods have to adopt that would help to enhance the biosynthesis of secondary products, so that prevention of further loss of plants can be augmented with yield. The work on secondary metabolites representing one or other biological properties has been reviewed by Bell (1980), Bell and Charlwood (1980); Luckner (1980); Balandrin *et al.* (1985) and Balandrin and Klocke (1988). The cell growth and secondary metabolites both can be manipulated by changing the media and culture conditions. Increase in yields has been observed in systematic studies that were based on biosynthetic pathways and localization of secondary metabolites (Shuler *et al.*, 1984; Staba, 1985).

The accumulation of secondary products in plant cell cultures is in response to deliberate treatments to the chemical and physical microenvironment. Secondary products can now be successfully accumulated in many undifferentiated plant cell cultures. Metabolite production *in vitro* also provides an excellent form for in-depth investigation of plant metabolic pathways under highly controlled conditions.

3. MATERIALS AND METHODS

Experimental materials

Explant

Healthy (disease and pest free plants), and elite (2-3 year old) stolens of *Centella asiatica* were selected from natural strands of Kodaikkanal and Kolli hills, Tamil Nadu, India. Then the stolens were planted and established at Department garden of Bharathidasan University (Plate 1) that receives a mean annual rainfall ranging from 100 to 120 cm with an average temperature of 38° C. The pH of the garden soil is 8.2.

Sterilization

Healthy young twigs (10 - 15 cm long) were collected from Department garden during different months from plants of *C. asiatica*. Explants like shoot tip, axillary node, leaf, petiole, internode, seed and node (1 - 2 cm) were excised, washed under running tap water for 30 minutes and then surface sterilized with (70% V/V) alcohol for 30 seconds followed by 7 min. in a solution of mercuric chloride (0.1% W/V). The explants were finally rinsed 5 - 6 times (each 5 minutes duration) in sterile distilled water. The final explant size should be of 0.5 - 1.0 cm long. The sterilized explants were cultured on the nutrient medium for the various experiments.

Culture media

The composition of various media used in the present study such as Murashige and Skoog, 1962 (MS), Schenk and Hildebrandt medium (Schenk and Hildebrandt, 1972), Gamborg medium (B5) (Gamborg *et al.,* 1968) and modified MS (MS salts + B5 vitamins) medium (mMS), was given in Table 4.

Preparations of stock solution and storage

Stock solutions of different media ingredients were prepared in 10X/100 ml and stored in stoppered brown bottles under refrigerated conditions. The stock solutions were used within 30 days.

Appropriate quantities of the various stock solutions, sucrose, myo-inositol (100 mg/l, W/V) and growth regulators were added. The final volume was made up with the addition of distilled water. After thorough mixing, the pH of the medium was adjusted to 5.7 (using 0.1N sodium hydroxide or 0.1N hydrochloric acid) before gelling with agar (0.8%, W/V; bacteriological grade, Hi media, India). The molten agar medium was dispensed into culture tubes (Borosil, India) (25X150mm: 10 ml) and plugged tightly with non-absorbent cotton. The culture tubes were autoclaved at 104 kPa and 121°C for 20 minutes.

Culture conditions

Cultures were maintained in a culture room at 25 ± 2°C under 16 h photoperiod provided by cool white fluorescent light (35 $\mu Em^{-2}S^{-1}$) with 55-65% relative humidity.

MICROPROPAGATION

Selection and inoculation of explants

The shoot tip of 6 - 8 mm length and the axillary nodal segments of 1 - 1.5 cm in length were excised from 2-3 years old-field grown plants, for micropropagation. Sterilized explants were placed on vertically on the nutrient medium containing different combinations of growth regulators.

Shoot proliferation

MS medium with 3% sucrose was supplemented cytokinins- 0.5 - 5.0 mg/l (BAP) or 0.5 - 6.0 mg/l (KN) either individually or in combination with various auxins (NAA, IBA and IAA: 0.1 - 1.0 mg/l) to optimize salt and growth regulators requirements for bud sprouting.

Shoot multiplication

Primary shoots formed *in vitro* were isolated and sectioned to one node pieces after removing the leaves. These nodal segments, each containing one axillary bud, were cultured on MS medium fortified with BAP (4.0 mg/l) + KN (5.0 mg/l) + auxins (IBA, IAA and NAA: 0.1 - 1.0 mg/l) + additives (Ads: 5.0 - 10 mg/l and GA_3 0.1 - 1.0 mg/l) + complex extracts (coconut milk: 5 - 15 % (V/V) and casein hydrolysate: 10 - 40 %) and sucrose (1.0 - 4.0 % (W/V)) for shoot multiplication. Subsequent subcultures were on the same medium at periodic intervals of 3 weeks. The morpogenic response in different seasons (January - December) and explant type (shoot tip and axillary node) were also investigated for effective, efficient and reproducible multiplication.

Shoot elongation

Proliferated multiple shoots were divided into small clusters of 1 - 2 shoots. They were subcultured on the same multiplication medium as described above.

Root induction

Shoots (6 - 7 cm length) formed *in vitro* were excised and transferred to half strength MS basal medium supplemented with 0.1-3.0 mg/l NAA, IBA and IAA in combination with 0.5 mg/l KN and 10.0 mg/l activated charcoal for rooting.

Acclimatization and hardening of plantlets

Well-rooted plantlets were removed from the culture medium and the roots were washed under running tap water to remove agar. The plantlets were transferred to plastic containers (5 cm diameter) containing red soil and vermiculate (1:3) and maintained at 25 ± 2°C, 16 h day length (35 - 50 $\mu Em^{-2}S^{-1}$) and 75 - 80% relative humidity. The potted plantlets were irrigated with 1/8 strength MS medium basal salts solution devoid of sucrose and myo-inositol, every 4 d for a period of 2 weeks. The plants were then transplanted to earthenware pots (10 cm diameter) containing natural soil and kept under shade for another 2 weeks. The potted plants were then placed outdoors under full sun.

ORGANOGENESIS

Explants viz. internode, petiole, leaf, seed and node were excised from 2 - 3 yrs field grown plant and cultured on a medium containing various growth regulators, after sterilization for organogenesis.

Callus induction

Various explants after sterilization, were cultured on MS basal medium containing 3% (W/V) sucrose, supplemented with various auxins, concentrations of 2,4-D, NAA, IBA and IAA (0.1, 0.5, 1.0, 2.0 and 3.0 mg/l) in combination with BAP (0.5 mg/l), for callus induction. Callus induction was observed from 15 - 20 days.

Shoot bud regeneration and shoot multiplication

Well-developed calli were transferred to shoot bud regeneration medium containing MS basal medium, 3% (W/V) sucrose, different concentrations of BAP (0.1, 0.5, 1.0, 2.0 and 3.0 mg/l) in combination with 0.5 mg/l of various auxins (NAA, 2,4-D, IBA and IAA individually) for shoot bud regeneration. Shoot bud differentiation was observed from 20 - 25 days of culture. Then these shoot buds were separated from callus and subcultured on shoot bud multiplication medium containing various concentrations of 2ip or BAP (0.5, 1.0, 2.0, 3.0 and 4.0 mg/l) in combination with 0.5 mg/l of NAA for further growth and multiple shoot bud formation. The masses of shoot initials were observed from 20 - 25 days of culture.

Shoot elongation

For shoot elongation regenerated shoot buds were subcultured on the same multiplication medium as described in organogenesis shoot bud regeneration and shoot multiplication.

Root induction

The elongated shoots (5-7 cm length) were transferred to half strength MS basal medium containing 3% (W/V) sucrose, different concentrations of NAA or IBA (0.1, 0.5, 1.0, 2.0 and 3.0 mg/l) in combination with 0.5 mg/l KN and 10.0 mg/l (W/V) activated charcoal (AC) for root initiation. Rooting was observed from 10 - 15 days of culture. Plantlets with well-developed roots were removed from the culture tubes and after washing their roots in running tap water; they were grown in vermiculate and red soil 3:1 ratio in the plastic cups for 15 days and subsequently transferred to pots.

Acclimatization and hardening of plantlets

Plantlets were kept for a week in the plastic containers at controlled temperature (24 ± 2°C) with 60% relative humidity, later on transfer to field conditions.

Statistical analysis

The experimental design was completely randomized design and factorial with auxin and cytokinin as independent variables. All the experiments were repeated five times. The data pertaining to frequencies of callus induction, shoot buds differentiation, shoot multiplication, root initiation and number shoots/culture were subjected to analysis of variance and mean separation was carried out using Duncan's Multiple Range Test (DMRT). Significance was determined at the 5% level (Gomez and Gomez, 1976).

Calculations

The experimental results were calculated as follows:

$$\text{Frequency of callus induction} : \frac{\text{No. of explants responded}}{\text{No. of explants plated}} \times 100$$

$$\text{Frequency of shoot bud regeneration} : \frac{\text{No. of calli regenerated}}{\text{No. of calli cultured}} \times 100$$

$$\text{Frequency of root induction} : \frac{\text{No. of shoots rooted}}{\text{No. of shoots cultured}} \times 100$$

SOMATIC EMBRYOGENESIS

Leaf and petiole segments, collected from 2 - 3 years old field grown plants, were used as the source for somatic embryogenesis experiments.

Callus induction

Solid MS basal medium containing MS vitamins, 0.8% agar (W/V), 3% (W/V) sucrose and 2,4-D (0.1-3.0 mg/l) was used for callus induction and explants were placed horizontally on the medium. The leaf explants were cut into 1.0 cm bits, which included the midrib. These leaf bits were placed either abaxial or adaxial surface down in 25 X 150 mm tubes containing 15 ml solid MS medium. The explants responded were subcultured at an interval of 30 days on the MS medium with different concentrations of 2,4-D (0.1 - 3.0 mg/l).

Induction of somatic embryos on solid medium

Fifteen days old whitish yellow friable calli were cultured on induction medium containing various concentrations of NAA or 2,4-D (1.0 - 4.0 mg/l) in combination with BAP (0.1 - 2.0 mg/l). At the end of 30 days, percentage of callus with somatic embryogenesis (calli with globular and later stages of embryos visible to naked eye and microscopically) was recorded.

Development and maturation of somatic embryos

Globular embryos formed after 30 days of culture were separated and transferred to MS basal medium augmented with NAA (0.5 mg/l) and different concentrations of KN (0.1 - 3.0 mg/l) for further development and maturation of somatic embryos, while MS basal medium lacking growth regulators served as the control.

Conversion of somatic embryos into plantlets

Fully developed cotyledonary stage somatic embryos were transferred to MS medium (3% sucrose) with different concentrations of BAP (0.1 - 3.0 mg/l), NAA (0.5 mg/l) and of activated charcoal (10.0mg/l) for germination and conversion into plantlets.

Development of plantlets

Fully germinated somatic embryos with well developed root and shoot systems were transferred in the same medium for further growth. Total number of plantlets with well-developed root and shoot systems were counted. The ratio of plantlets formed to the total number of germinated embryos was calculated as the conversion percentage.

Suspension cultures

Fifteen days old whitish yellow friable and yellowish brown less compact calli (1 g fresh weight), were aseptically transferred to 150 ml Erlemeyer flask containing 50 ml of MS basal liquid medium without agar, 3% (W/V) sucrose, 2,4-D (1.0 - 5.0 mg/l) and BAP (1.0 mg/l). The suspension was agitated on a shaker (100 - 110 rmp). Further subculters involved in the replacement of 10 ml of the cell suspension with fresh medium of the same formulation at 10 days interval. Cultures were filtered through 125 μm stainless steel sieves to separate individual cells and small cell clumps. Cells from the suspension were observed with a microscope during the culture period and the growth of cells was monitored from the 15th day by determining the packed cell volume (PCV) of samples from 10 replicates. Embryos at different stages of development were separated manually.

Development of somatic embryos

Globular stage embryos, which formed after 15 days in MS liquid medium, were subcultured on MS liquid medium containing NAA (1.0 - 4.0 mg/l) in combination with BAP (0.1 - 2.0 mg/l) for further development. After 12 days of subculture, heart shaped embryos were formed from globular stage embryos. After a period of further growth, heart shaped embryos were separated and subcultured in the same medium for development of torpedo shaped embryos.

Germination of somatic embryos

The torpedo stage embryos were transferred to MS liquid medium having 3% (W/V) sucrose, BAP (0.1 - 3.0 mg/l) in combination with NAA (0.5 mg/l) and activated charcoal (AC) (10.0 mg/l) for germination and conversion into plantlets.

Development of plantlets

Fully germinated somatic embryos with well developed root and shoot systems were transferred to MS medium with 0.8% (W/V) agar for further growth. The sucrose content was kept at 3% (W/V). Total number of plantlets with well-developed root and shoot systems were counted. The ratio of plantlets formed to the total number of germinated embryos was calculated as the conversion percentage.

Acclimatization and hardening of plantlets

Complete plantlets with well-developed roots in the culture tubes were subjected to the following hardening procedure. After removing the cotton plugs, the plantlets were removed from the tubes and washed in the running tap water. Thereafter, the plantlets were transferred to the plastic containers containing red soil and vermiculate 1:3 and later established in pots.

Photomicrograph

Samples were photographed at different stages of growth periods using Nikon FX-35 camera (Japan make).

Statistical analysis

The experimental design was completely randomized design and factorial with auxin and cytokinin as independent variables. All the experiments were repeated five times with 25 replications of each treatment. The data pertaining to somatic embryogenesis was subjected to analysis of variance and mean separation was carried out using Duncan's Multiple Range Test (DMRT). Significance was determined at the 5% level (Gomez and Gomez, 1976).

Calculations

The experimental results were calculated as follows:

$$\text{Percentage of embryogenesis} : \frac{\text{No. of explants showing embryogenic cells}}{\text{Total no. of explants plated}} \times 100$$

$$\text{Maturation response} : \frac{\text{No. of mature embryos formed}}{\text{No. of embryogenic calli cultured}} \times 100$$

PHYTOCHEMICAL ANALYSIS

Two different plant materials, leaf and callus, were selected for preliminary phytochemical analysis. Leaf material was collected from 2 - 3 years old-field grown plants, whereas callus was from *in vitro* conditions. Regenerated callus was obtained from different explants (leaf, petiole, internode, seed and node) on MS medium containing various concentrations of NAA (0.1 2.0 mg/l), 2,4-D (0.1 - 2.0 mg/l) either individually or in combination with BAP (0.5 - 3.0 mg/l) and KN (0.1 - 3.0 mg/l). Both materials were dried at room temperature (33 ° C) and made into powder for further analysis.

Various organic solvents, petroleum ether, benzene, chloroform, ethyl acetate, acetone, butanol, ethanol and methanol, were used to extract leaf and callus powder through soxhlet apparatus as follows (Brindha *et al.*, 1977 and Kokat, 1995):

Petroleum ether extract

The coarse powder (leaf and callus) was extracted with 1.0 l of petroleum ether by continuous hot percolation (60 - 80°C) using soxhlet apparatus until the extraction was completed (24 hours). After completion of extraction the extract was filtered and concentrated to dryness under reduced pressure. A yellowish dark green residue was obtained.

Benzene extract

The marc after petroleum ether extraction was dried and extracted with 1.0 l of benzene by continuous hot percolation (79 - 81°C) for 24 hours until the extraction was completed. After the completion of the extraction, the extract was filtered and the solvent was removed by distillation under reduced pressure. A dark green colored residue was obtained.

Chloroform extract

The marc left after the benzene extraction was dried and extracted with 1.0 l of chloroform by continuous hot percolation (59 - 61°C) until the extraction was completed. After completion of the extraction, the extract was filtered and the solvent was removed by distillation under reduced pressure. A dark green coloured residue was obtained.

Ethyl acetate extract

The marc after chloroform extraction was dried and extracted with 1.0 l of ethyl acetate by continuous hot percolation (60 - 70°C) for 24 hours until the extraction was completed. After the completion of the extraction, the extract was filtered and the solvent was removed by distillation under reduced pressure. A dark green coloured residue was obtained.

Acetone extract

The marc left after the chloroform extraction was dried and extracted with 1.0 l of acetone by continuous hot percolation (55 - 56°C) until the extraction was completed. After the completion of the extraction, the extract was filtered and the solvent was removed by distillation under reduced pressure. A dark green coloured residue was obtained.

Butanol extract

The marc left after the acetone extraction was dried and extracted with 1.0 l of butanol (60 - 80°C) by continuous hot percolation using soxhlet apparatus until the extraction was completed (24 hours). After completion of extraction, the extract was filtered and concentrated to dryness under reduced pressure. A brownish dark green coloured residue was obtained.

Alcohol extract

The marc left after the butanol extraction was dried and extracted with 1.0 liters of ethanol (60 - 65°C) 95% by continuous hot percolation, until the extraction was completed. After the completion of the extraction, it was filtered and the solvent was removed by distillation under reduced pressure. A light green coloured residue was obtained.

SCREENING TESTS

Secondary metabolites, such as steroids, triterpenoids, alkaloids, phenolic compounds, tannins, saponins, xanthoproteins, flavonoids, essential oils, volatile oils, and carbohydrates were screened by the methods described by Brindha *et al.* (1977) and Kokate, (1995) as follows: The methods of preliminary photochemical analysis have been presented. Using the methods of as follows:

1) Alkaloids

The extracts were treated with Mayer's reagent to test the presence or absence of alkaloids. White precipitate or turbidity indicates the presence of alkaloids.

2) Volatile oils

5 ml of solution was evaporated on a porcelain crucible. If the residue had an aromatic smell, it indicates the presence of volatile oils.

3) Fatty acids

Two ml of the solution was evaporated on a filter paper. A translucent spot indicates the presence of fatty acids.

4) Emodins

To the few ml of extract(s) solution 25% (W/V) ammonium hydroxide solution was added. The appearance of red colour indicated the presence of emodins.

5) Flavanoids

The extract(s) was treated with concentrated hydrochloric acid. Then 200 mg of magnesium metal powder was added. The appearance of pink magenta or red colour indicated the presence of flavonoids.

6) Steroids/triterpenoids (Libermann-Burchard Reaction)

Few ml of all the extracts were evaporated and the residues were dissolved in 0.5ml glacial acetic acid, followed by the addition of 0.5 ml of chloroform and a few drops of concentrated sulfuric acid. The appearance of green and red-violet colour indicated the presence of steroids and triterpenes respectively.

7) Antharacene glycosides

The appearance of red colour on the addition of 25% (W/V) ammonium hydroxide to the extract(s) indicated the presence of antharacene glycosides.

8) Phenolics

Few ml of extract(s) were treated with 2 ml of water. To which 4 drops of ferric chloride ($FeCl_3$) reagent was added. The developed blue colour indicated the presence of phenolics.

9) Saponins (Forth Test)

Few ml of all extracts were shaken with 5 ml of distilled water in a test tube. Appearance of foam indicated the presence of saponins.

10) Tannins

Few ml of all the extracts were treated with 2 ml of distilled water. Then the solution was tested with the followings reagents.

Reagent	Inference
1. $FeCl_3$ solution	Appearance of blue, bluish black or bluish green colour
2. Lead acetate test	Appearance of white or brownish yellow
3. Gelatin solution	Appearance of turbidity

11) Xanthoprotein

Few ml of all the extracts were treated with nitric acid. Then a few drops of liquid drops of liquid ammonia were added. Formation of reddish orange (or) reddish pink colour indicated the presence of xanthoprotein.

12) Carbohydrates

To few ml of all the extracts 1 ml of 10% (W/V) sodium hydroxide solution was added and headed formation of brown colour indicated the presence of carbohydrates.

4. RESULTS

MICROPROPAGATION

Shoot tip and axillary node explants were selected and grown on MS medium supplemented with various growth regulators for micropropagation.

Effect of plant growth regulators

Shoot tip and axillary node sprouting was initiated at all concentrations of BAP and KN (alone and in combinations). MS medium containing BAP was more effective than KN for inducing proliferation of axillary nodes. Shoots developed longer internodes on BAP fortified medium than on KN supplemented medium. Both BAP (4.0 mg/l) and KN (5.0 mg/l) in the culture medium promoted the highest shoot sprouting and multiple shoot induction. KN did not improve significantly the shoot length and the number of proliferating shoots. Superiority of BAP and KN in combination was found for bud break and shoot multiplication in axillary bud explants. KN and BAP at higher concentrations (<5.0 mg/l) resulted in suppression of shoot sprouting and domination of callus growth (Table 5). The shoot number was increased when auxins (NAA, IAA and IBA at 0.5 mg/l) combined with optimized BAP and KN (Table 6). Auxin combined with either BAP or KN alone resulted in low propagation rate (data not shown). Though both NAA and IBA increased the shoot number, NAA (0.5 mg/l) showed the highest overall growth response in both shoot tip and axillary nodes (Table 6) (Plate 1, Fig. a and plate 2, Fig. a).

Additives

MS medium containing the optimum level of auxin and cytokinin in combinations of Ads and GA_3 were used for the multiple shoot bud induction and to improve the quality of shoots. A combination of optimal concentration of Ads (10.0 mg/l) and GA_3 (0.5 mg/l) in the culture medium not only induced a faster bud break but also enhanced the frequency of bud break 78% and 83% in shoot tip and axillary node respectively (Table 7). In addition, Ads and GA_3 coupling had a synergistic effect on multiple shoot formation (8.6 shoots/explant and 9.2 shoots/explant) in shoot tip and axillary nodes) as well as on internode elongation (4.92 cm and 5.88 cm in shoot tip and axillary nodes respectively) (Table 7).

Complex extracts

Synergistic effect of complex extract and was studied the optimum cytokinin, auxin and additives levels for shoot sprouting and to improve the quality of the shoots. CM (10%) enhanced the shoot number (14.6 shoots/explant and 18.8 shoots/explant in shoot tip and axillary node respectively). CH (30%) also enhanced the shoot number both in shoot tip and axillary node explants. CM and CH addition prevented the yellowing of leaves and reduced the callus formation at the cut end of the shoots (Table 8). Increase in the concentration of CM (above 10%) and CH (above 30%) resulted in callusing and suppression of shoot bud proliferation. Thus CM (10%) was found to be necessary for speedy proliferation of shoot buds and to improve the quality and quantity of shoots in both explants (Plate 2, Fig. b and Plate 3, Fig. b)

Sucrose

Sucrose at 3% level enhanced bud break, shoot number and shoot length considerably. Sucrose levels above and below 3% showed decline in shoot proliferation, leaves turned yellow and shoots become slender (Table 9).

Seasons

The temporal changes have influence on the response of mature axillary node explants *in vitro*. Hence, continuous trials using axillary node explants from mature plants throughout the year were maintained on MS medium containing optimized plant growth regulators and adjuvants. Multiple shoot regeneration gradually increased from May - November in axillary node explants (Table 10). Maximum frequency of shoots and bud sprouting was observed formed from axillary node explants collected during the months of September to November. After that, the shoot number and response declined. The next best season is from July to August.

Explant

Among the explants tested, axillary node explant showed positive morphogenetic response and readily developed multiple shoots, whereas shoot tip explants produced basal callus (Table 11). The maximum shoot bud sprouting (92%) and shoot number (19.8 shoots/explant) without callus formation occurred in axillary node explants.

Subculturing of *in vitro* produced shoots

During the multiplication stage, the new shoots when cut into segments contained one or two nodes and cultured in the same medium gave rise to new shoots. In addition, when the original axillary node was cultured (after removal of the multiple shoots to stem), the number of shoots increased for the next 2 - 3 subcultures and reduced thereafter. Hence from the single node explant it was possible to obtain a significant number of new shoots within a period of 3 months (data not shown).

Medium

Shoot tips and axillary nodes remained green and fresh bud failed to sprout on any media without growth regulators. Among the 4 different media tested, MS medium was found to be the best basal medium for shoot sprouting (78.8% and 84.4% in shoot tip and axillary node respectively), number (8.4 and 9.2 shoots/explant in shoot tip and axillary node respectively) and shoot length (4.88 and 5.92 cm in shoot tip and axillary node respectively) followed by mMS, B_5 and SH media (Table 12).

Rooting induction

Elongated shoots produced from both shoot tip and axillary node explants failed to root on half strength MS medium without any growth regulator supplement. Addition of auxin to the culture medium induced rooting in both explants. Of the three auxins tested, NAA at (2.0 mg/l) in combination with KN (0.5 mg/l) and activated charcoal (10.0 mg/l) was most effective in inducing roots in 89% and 95% in shoot tip and axillary node respectively followed by 2.0 mg/l IBA in 73% and 86% in shoot tip and axillary node respectively (Table 13). IAA showed little response (Plate 2, Fig. c and Plate 3, Fig. c).

Acclimatization and hardening of plantlets

Plantlets (6 - 7 cm long) with 4 - 5 fully expanded leaves and well-developed roots were successfully transferred to plastic container containing red soil and vermiculate (1:3) and kept at 25 ± 2° C for 2 weeks. The plantlets were then transferred earthen pots containing red soil and vermiculite (1:3), for another 2 weeks and the potted plants were then placed under shade. Later potted plants were transferred to the field conditions. About 80 - 85% of the plants survived during the transfer from *in vitro* and *in vivo* conditions. Normal growth of the potted plants was visible 15 - 20 days after transfer to field condition. The transplantation success was about 80 - 85%. The regenerated plants of both the explants did not show any detectable variation in morphological or growth characteristics when compared with the donor plants (Plate 2, Fig. d and Plate 3, Fig. d).

ORGANOGENESIS

The response of different explants viz. internode, petiole, leaf, seed and node of *C.asiatica* for organogenesis via callus at various concentrations of auxin and cytokinin combination of Murashige and Skoog (MS) (1962) medium was as follows (Table 14 - 19).

Internode

Internode explants derived from 2 - 3 years old field grown plants of *C.asiatica* were grown on MS basal medium was supplemented with different concentrations of 2,4-D, NAA, IBA and IAA (0.1 - 3.0 mg/l) in combination with BAP (1.0 mg/l) for callus initiation. The explants enlarged and produced green callus from the cut end. Callus growth was the best in the presence of 2,4-D (2.0 mg/l) followed by NAA, IBA and IAA (Table 14). There were statistically significant differences observed between percent of callus induction and various auxin types per responding culture ($p<0.05$ for each auxin). The highest frequency of callus induction (100%) was observed within 15 days on MS basal medium containing 2.0 mg/l 2,4-D and 1.0 mg/l BAP, which was highly significant at 5% level.

The calli were transferred to shoot bud regeneration medium containing different concentrations of BAP (0.5 - 3.0 mg/l) in combination with various auxins NAA, 2,4-D, IBA and IAA (0.5 mg/l) for shoot bud differentiation (Table 15). Addition of BAP suppressed callus formation and induced shoot bud differentiation. Internode-derived calli produced shoot bud primorda and these shoot buds developed into normal shoots after 20 days of culture. The highest frequency of shoot bud regeneration (100%) was observed on MS basal medium supplemented with BAP (2.0 mg/l) and NAA (0.5 mg/l) combination, after 20 days of culture (Table 15). These shoot buds were cultured on shoot bud multiplication medium containing various concentrations of BAP or 2ip (0.5 - 4.0 mg/l) in combination with NAA (0.5 mg/l). 2ip had significant correlation with the number of shoots as well as frequency of shooting per responding culture ($p<0.05$). The mean number of shoots was increased with increase in the concentration of cytokinin and the highest number of shoots (59 shoots/culture) was observed on MS medium supplemented with 3.0 mg/l 2ip and 0.5 mg/l NAA combination, after 20 days of culture (Table 16). Well-developed shoots

(5 - 7 cm long) were isolated from the culture tubes and transferred to rooting medium supplemented with half strength MS medium supplemented with different concentrations of NAA or IBA (0.5 - 3.0 mg/l), KN (0.5 mg/l) and activated charcoal (10 mg/l) for root formation. The highest frequency of rooting (95%) was observed on a half strength MS medium containing 2.0 mg/l NAA + 0.5 mg/l KN and 10 mg/l of AC combination within 15 days of culture (Table 17). The percentage of rooting increased with the increase in the concentration of auxin upto 2.0 mg/l, further increase in auxin concentration decrease the rooting response. Thus a significant correlation was observed between auxin concentration and rooting response ($p<0.05$). The regenerated plantlets were transferred to plastic cups containing vermiculite and red soil (3:1) and subsequently established in the pots and grown till maturity (Plate 4, Fig. a - g).

Petiole

Petiole explants were subjected to MS basal medium containing different concentrations of 2,4-D, NAA, IBA and IAA (0.1 - 3.0 mg/l) in combination with 1.0 mg/l BAP for callus initiation. The petiole explants began to enlarge on medium within 7 days of culture, callus developed from the cut end of the explants and became green in colour. Among the various concentrations of auxins, 2,4-D (2.0 mg/l) + BAP (1.0 mg/l) was found to be the best for highest frequency of callus initiation (100%) followed by 2.0 mg/l NAA (80%), 2.0 mg/l IBA (76%) and 2.0 mg/l IAA (71%) after 15 days of culture (Table 14). The callus was compact and did not regenerate plants on the same medium. Auxin type had a significant effect on the frequency of callus induction per responding explant ($p<0.05$).

After one month, these calli were transferred to shoot bud regeneration medium {MS medium augmented with different concentrations of BAP (0.1-3.0 mg/l) along with 0.5 mg/l of various auxins (2,4-D, NAA, IBA and IAA)}. Proliferation of shoot initials was observed after 20 days of culture, with little callusing. Within 10 days of culture initiation, 100% of the petiole-derived calli formed shoot buds. The highest shoot bud formation was obtained in 2.0 mg/l BAP and 0.5 mg/l NAA combination, after 20 days of culture (Table 15). There was significant correlation between BAP treatment and shoot bud regeneration frequency ($p<0.05$). The percentage of shooting from petiole derived calli varied with different concentrations of BAP along with various auxin combinations. After shoot differentiation, they were cultured on multiple shoot induction medium, which was supplemented with different concentrations of cytokinins (BAP or 2ip 0.5 - 4.0 mg/l) in combination with 0.5 mg/l NAA. The highest number of multiple shoots (49 shoots/culture) was observed on MS basal medium fortified with 3.0 mg/l 2ip and 0.5 mg/l NAA combination after 20 days of culture (Table 16). Elongated shoots (5 - 7 cm long) were excised and cultured on half strength MS medium supplemented with different concentrations of NAA or IBA (0.1 - 3.0 mg/l) in combination with 0.5 mg/l KN and 10.0 mg/l AC for rooting. Roots emerged from the cut ends of the shoots in 90% of the cultures within 15 days. Of the two auxins tested, NAA (2.0 mg/l) + KN (0.5 mg/l) and AC (10.0 mg/l) combinations was found to be the superior for highest frequency of rooting than IBA (2.0 mg/l) + KN (1.0 mg/l) and AC (10 mg/l) combination (Table 17). Auxin type and concentration on rooting response was highly significant at 5% level. The rooted plantlets have been transferred initially to plastic container containing vermiculite and red soil (3:1) established in the pots and grown to maturity (Plate 5, Fig. a - g).

Leaf

The leaf explants enlarged to twice their original size, and also formed greenish, compact callus on MS basal medium supplemented with 2,4-D, NAA, IBA and IAA (0.1 - 3.0 mg/l) in combination with BAP (1.0 mg/l) after 15 days of culture initiation. The highest frequency of callus initiation (100%) was observed on a medium containing 2.0 mg/l 2,4-D and 1.0 mg/l of BAP followed by NAA (76%), IBA (74%) and IAA (66%) (Table 14). Statistical analysis performed for each auxin to determine the effect of concentration on callus initiation was significant at 5% level. These calli were subcultured on MS basal medium containing various concentrations of BAP (0.1 - 3.0 mg/l) with different auxins (0.5 mg/l) individually for shoot bud differentiation. The highest shoot bud differentiation (100%) was observed on MS basal medium containing BAP (2.0 mg/l) and NAA (0.5 mg/l) after 20 days of culture (Table 15). These shoot buds were transferred to multiple shooting medium.

Multiple shoots were produced on MS basal medium supplemented with different concentrations of BAP or 2ip (0.5 - 4.0 mg/l) and NAA (0.5 mg/l), after 20 days of culture. Statistical analysis showed significant correlation between cytokinin concentration and shooting response per responding culture ($p<0.05$). The highest number of shoots (40 shoots/culture) was observed on a medium augmented with 3.0 mg/l 2ip in combination with 0.5 mg/l NAA (Table 16). These shoots were separated and transferred to half strength MS basal medium supplemented with various concentrations of NAA or IBA (0.1 - 3.0 mg/l) in combination with 0.5 mg/l KN and 10 mg/l AC. The highest frequency of root formation (86%) was observed on the medium containing 2.0 mg/l NAA + 1.0 mg/l KN and 10% AC, after 15 of culture mg/l (Table 17). In the present study, auxins had a significant effect on the rooting frequency ($p<0.05$). The rooted plantlets were transferred initially to plastic container containing vermiculite and red soil (3:1) and subsequently established in pots and grown successfully (Plate 6, Fig. a - f).

Seed

Immature seed explants were cultured on MS basal medium containing different concentrations of 2,4-D, NAA, IBA and IAA (0.1 -3.0 mg/l) in combination with BAP (1.0 mg/l) for callus initiation. The combination of 2,4-D (2.0 mg/l) and BAP (1.0 mg/l) was found to be the most efficient for high frequency of callus induction (93%) followed by NAA (67%), IBA (71%) and IAA (65%), after15 days of culture (Table 14). In the present study, statistical analysis revealed significant correlation between auxin concentration and callus induction frequency at 5% level. After 30 days, these calli were subcultured on shoot bud regeneration medium containing different concentrations of BAP (0.1 - 3.0 mg/l) in combination with NAA, 2,4-D, IBA and IAA (0.5 mg/l). Proliferation of shoot initials was observed after 20 days of culture, with little callusing. BAP and NAA combination was found to be the best for high frequency of shoot bud differentiation (88%) within 20 days of culture (Table 15).

These shoot buds produced the maximum number of multiple shoots on MS basal medium containing BAP or 2ip (3.0 mg/l) and NAA (0.5 mg/l) combination which was highly significant at 5% level. Multiple shoot number was higher (32.3 shoots/culture) in 2ip (3.0 mg/l) + NAA (0.5 mg/l) combination, whereas it was 22.4 shoots/culture in BAP (3.0 mg/l) + NAA (0.5 mg/l) combination after 20 days of culture (Table 16). The statistical analysis revealed a significant correlation between 2ip concentration and shooting response ($p<0.05$). After a month, the elongated shoots (5 - 7 cm long) were excised and transferred to half strength MS basal medium supplemented with different concentrations of NAA or IBA (0.1 - 3.0 mg/l) in combination with KN (0.5 mg/l) and AC (10 mg/l) for rooting. Roots were emerged from the cut end of the shoots after 15 days of culture. NAA (2.0 mg/l) + KN (0.5 mg/l) and AC (10 mg/l) combination was found to be the best (80%) for highest frequency of rooting with numerous lateral roots followed by IBA (2.0 mg/l) + KN (0.5 mg/l) and AC (10 mg/l) combination was found to the best (80%) for highest frequency of rooting with numerous lateral roots followed by IBA (2.0 mg/l) + KN (0.5 mg/l) + AC (10.0 mg/l) combination (70%) (Table 17). In the present study, auxin type and concentration showed a significant effect on rooting frequency per responding culture ($p<0.05$). The rooted shoots were transferred initially to the plastic container and later established in pots and grown to maturity (Plate 7, Fig. a - g).

Node

The node explants (0.5 - 1.0 cm long) were cultured on MS basal medium containing different concentrations of 2,4-D, NAA, IBA and IAA (0.1 - 3.0 mg/l) in combination with BAP (1.0 mg/l) resulted in callus induction after 15 days of culture initiation. The highest frequency of callus initiation (86%) was observed on a medium containing 2.0 mg/l 2,4-D and 1.0 mg/l BAP followed by NAA (65%), IBA (67%) and IAA (61%) (Table 14). Statistical analysis performed for each auxin to determine the effect of concentration of callus initiation were significant at 5% level. These compact, green colour calli were subcultured on MS basal medium containing various concentrations of BAP (0.1 - 3.0 mg/l) with different auxins NAA, 2,4-D, IBA and IAA (0.5 mg/l) individually for shoot bud differentiation. Proliferation of shoot initials from the callus after 20 days of culture initiation, developed into shoot buds with little callusing. BAP (2.0 mg/l) and NAA (0.5 mg/l) combination was found to be the best for high frequency of shoot bud differentiation (81%) after 20 days of culture (Table 15). In the present study, BAP concentrations significantly correlated with shoot bud formation per responding culture ($p<0.05$). Multiple shoot buds developed from the region of the protuberance, which developed further into shoots after 20 days of culture. Multiple shoots were induced on MS basal medium containing various concentrations of BAP or 2ip (0.5 - 4.0 mg/l) and NAA (0.5 mg/l). The highest number of shoots (24 shoots/culture) observed on MS basal medium containing 3.0 mg/l 2ip and 0.5 mg/l NAA combination and it was only 21.8 shoots/culture in BAP (3.0 mg/l) and 0.5 mg/l NAA combination (Table 16). Little callus was formed at the basal part of the bud. The isolated shoots were transferred to half strength MS basal medium supplemented with NAA or IBA (0.1 - 3.0 mg/l) in combination with KN (0.5 mg/l) and AC (10 mg/l) for rooting. The highest frequency of rooting (72%) was observed on a medium containing NAA (2.0 mg/l) + KN (0.5 mg/l) and AC (10 mg/l) combination, whereas it was 65% in IBA (2.0 mg/l) + KN (1.0 mg/l) and AC (10 mg/l) after 15 days of culture (Table 17). Statistical analysis showed a significant difference between rooting frequency and auxin type at 5% level. The rooted plantlets were initially transferred to plastic container, subsequently established in pots (Plate 8, Fig. a - g).

Invariably all the above explants were failed to show any morphogenetic changes when cultured on MS medium lacking plant growth regulators.

Medium

The effect of different types of media was examined for their ability to support organogenesis. The high percentage of organogenic potential in MS media proved to be the most efficient in supporting callus growth and organogenic potential in *C.asiatica* followed by mMS, SH and B5 media. This shows the differential requirement of basic nutrients (Table 18).

Effect of auxins

The influence of the auxin was examined by culturing the explants for 15 days on MS medium containing different concentrations of 2,4-D, NAA, IBA and IAA (0.5 - 3.0 mg/l). The effect of 2,4-D and NAA were found to be similar and resulted in high percentage of (100%) callus formation, while IAA and IBA treated explants produced callus with less percentage (81%) (Table 14). 2,4-D, NAA, IBA and IAA at 0.5 mg/l concentrations increased the shooting percentage (Table 15). Of the four auxins tested, 2,4-D was found to be the most effective for callus induction followed by NAA, IBA and IAA, whereas NAA was found to be the superior for shoot bud regeneration as well as shoot multiplication and root initiation (Table 16 and 17). IBA was found to be more efficient than IAA for callus induction, shoot initiation shoot multiplication and rooting. NAA was found to be superior to IBA for rooting.

Effect of cytokinins

Since maximum number of shoot buds per culture was observed with 3.0 mg/l cytokinin (2ip or BAP) in all cultures, this concentration was chosen to study the comparative response of two cytokinins. Both 2ip and BAP favored multiple shoot bud development from shoot bud cultures. However, BAP not only induced differentiation of callus (100%) and shoot buds in 100% of the total cultures but also developed multiple shoots. The number of shoots per culture varied with cytokinin. 2ip was the most effective than BAP with regard to the number of shoots produced per explant.

Synergistic effect of auxins and cytokinins

When MS medium was supplemented with auxin, the explants produced callus, but the growth of callus was very poor and frequency of callusing was low (Data not shown). Therefore, a very low concentration of cytokinin (1.0 mg/l) was added to increase the frequency of callusing. Proliferation of shoot initials from the callus, in the presence of low concentration of auxin, suggests the cytokinin: auxin ratio is important for this response. The efficiency of 2ip or BAP on shoot bud multiplication was enhanced when it was supplemented with NAA. The regeneration response of callus increased significantly when auxin (0.5 mg/l) was added with cytokinin. The root induction frequency was also enhanced by low concentration of KN (0.5 mg/l).

Effect of explant

Of the 5 different explants tested, internode was found to be the best followed by petiole, leaf, seed and node explant for callus induction, shoot regeneration, shoot multiplication and rooting (Table 14 - 17). There was a qualitative variation in regeneration response between internode and other explants. The internode explant showed the highest frequency of callus initiation on MS + 2,4-D (2.0 mg/l) + BAP (1.0 mg/l), shoot bud differentiation on MS + NAA (0.5 mg/l) + BAP (2.0 mg/l), multiple shoot induction on MS + NAA (0.5 mg/l) + 2ip (3.0 mg/l) and root formation on half MS + NAA (2.0 mg/l) + KN (0.5 mg/l + AC (10.0 mg/l) (Table 19).

SOMATIC EMBRYOGENESIS

Callus Induction

Callus efficiency of petiole and leaf explants were tested on MS basal medium containing 2,4-D and NAA. Explants initiated callus after 15 days of inoculation. The callus covered the entire explant within a week. Of the two explants tested, petiole produced maximum induction of callus than leaf explants. Petiole explants produced whitish yellow and friable calli on 2.0 mg/l of 2,4-D and leaf explant produced yellowish brown and less compact calli on 2.0 mg/l 2,4-D. Among the two auxins used (2,4-D and NAA), 2,4-D induced maximum amount of friable callus (Table 20). In addition, prolonged culture period resulted in browning and death of callus (Plate 9, Fig. a and Plate 10, Fig. a).

Somatic embryogenesis on solid medium

Somatic embryogenesis was induced on MS medium supplemented with different concentrations of NAA and 2,4-D (0.1, 0.5, 1.0, 2.0, 3.0, 4.0 and 5.0 mg/l) in combination with BAP (1.0 mg/l). Embryogenesis was not observed on the basal medium without any growth regulator supplementations. While with NAA or 2,4-D in the medium, globular embryo like structures were observed from the 35 - 40 days culture. The effect of different auxins (2,4-D and NAA) on somatic embryogenesis was statistically significant at 5% level. Nodular structures were observed in most of the combinations with varied response. Hereafter, these nodular structures are referred as embryogenic masses, since the development of embryos were restricted to these protuberances. The frequency of embryogenic mass production varied with the types and concentrations of auxin used. The highest frequency of embryogenesis was (60%) and (80%) in NAA (3.0 mg/l) + BAP (1.0 mg/l) and 2,4-D (3.0 mg/l) + BAP (1.0 mg/l) combination respectively for petiole, where as in NAA (3.0 mg/l) + BAP (1.0 mg/l) and 2,4-D (3.0 mg/l) + BAP (1.0 mg/l) combinations the frequency was 50% and 70% respectively for leaf explant (Table 21) (Plate 9 and 10, Fig. band b) .

In general, more nodular structures appeared on media with a high ratio of 2,4-D. The analysis of data shows that the embryogenic mass induction was higher in 2,4-D at 3.0 mg/l and BAP (1.0 mg/l) combination, which was highly significant at 5% level. Thus, 3.0 mg/l of 2,4-D was selected as the optimum level for maximum frequency of somatic embryogenesis in both explants. In lower concentrations the initial hump formation was noted as low frequency but it associated with callusing. Similar observations were noted in NAA and BAP combinations also. At higher concentrations the initial embryogenic mass induction at low frequency was observed at the end of the fourth week, the growth was minimum and tissue became white. Various stages of embryos were observed in the same culture and its development was synchronous. Average number of embryos was also high (52 embryos/culture) in petiole at 3.0 mg/l 2,4-D and 1.0 mg/l BAP combination, while 46 embryos/culture were observed in leaf explant, after 25 days of culture (Table-21).

Somatic embryo development and maturation

Somatic embryos (globular shaped) were transferred to embryo development and maturation medium. Somatic embryos further developed into different stages within 25 days on the medium containing 0.5 mg/l NAA and different concentrations of KN (0.5 - 3.0 mg/l).

On the maturation medium the embryos were turned green and developed into mature embryos. MS basal medium with 2.0 mg/l of KN and 0.5 mg/l of NAA was found to be the best combination for maturation of embryos, after 20 days. Matured embryos were increased with increase in concentration of KN from 0.5 - 2.0 mg/l and the highest response was observed at 2.0 mg/l, which was highly significant at 5% level. However, medium with higher dose of KN (>2.0 mg/l) resulted in recallusing of the embryos. Maturation frequency was found to be higher (92%) in petiole explant, whereas it was 80% in leaf explants (Table 22). Statistical analysis revealed a significant correlation between KN concentration and maturation response in responding culture at 5% level (Plate 9 and 10 - Fig. c, d).

Conversion of somatic embryos into plantlets

Mature embryos from both the explants were transferred to germination medium containing 3% (W/V) sucrose, BAP (0.1 - 3.0 mg/l), 0.5 mg/l NAA and 10 mg/l AC. The frequency of embryo germination varied from 20% to 87% with varied response of shoots and roots development. For germination of embryos, MS basal medium with BAP (2.0 mg/l) + NAA (0.5 mg/l) and AC (10.0 mg/l) combinations were found to be more suitable and this combination was found to be significant at 5% level (Table-23). The embryo germination was also increased with increase in the BAP (0.1 - 2.0 mg/l), further increase of BAP (2.0 - 3.0 mg/l) concentrations decrease the embryo germination. A significant correlation was observed between BAP concentration and conversion frequency per responding culture. In general, lower concentration of auxin and higher concentration of cytokinin favored a higher conversion rate of somatic embryos into plantlets. Germination of embryos was characterized by simultaneous production of root and shoot systems. The germinated embryos developed into complete plantlets on the same medium after 15 days of culture (Table 23) (Plate 9 and 10 - Fig. e, f).

SOMATIC EMBRYOGENESIS IN LIQUID MEDIUM

Establishment of cell suspension cultures

The whitish yellow friable and yellowish brown, less compact callus was transferred to MS suspension medium containing different concentrations of 2,4-D (1.0 - 5.0 mg/l) and BAP (1.0 mg/l) for embryo initiation (Table 24). The dispersion of these calli produced a suspension mainly composed of free cells, small clusters of 15-20 cells and irregular aggregates. Most of the cells were arranged randomly on the callus, however, some globular organization of dividing cells occurred after three weeks.

Somatic embryo induction

The single cell stopped dividing and differentiated into large, curved and vacuolated cells. Some cells within the groups are small, relatively round, dense and often green. These cells kept dividing to form a compact, globular proembryonic masses. The whole embryo became round and green globular embryos. The frequency of somatic embryo induction was increased with increase the concentration of NAA in the medium and the highest frequency was observed at 3.0 mg/l of NAA in combination with 1.0 mg/l of KN (Table 25). The frequency of somatic embryo induction was 69.2% and 60.8% in callus derived from petiole and leaf explants respectively (Table 24). Statistical analysis has revealed a significant correlation between auxin concentration and embryo induction. They can be easily identified from undifferentiated aggregates as judged by their texture and colour. The developmental changes at more advanced stages as heart, torpedo and dicotyledonary shaped embryos were observed after the second subculture on the same medium (Table 25) (Plate 11 - Fig. a-e).

Plantlet development from somatic embryos

The heart and torpedo shaped embryos were transferred to germination medium supplemented with 3% (W/V) sucrose, NAA (0.5 mg/l) and BAP (2.0 mg/l) for further development. The torpedo shaped embryos of both the explants developed into cotyledonary stages in this medium after 20 days. The majority of cotyledonary embryos had fused cotyledons, which did not open. The shoot meristems with primary leaves did not emerge in such cases. Following placement of the mature embryos on the germination medium, hypocotyls and root elongation were first observed in 7 days. The majority of the embryos had undergone shoot elongation within 15 days. Cotyledon developments in these embryos were reduced and shoot elongation required an additional 15-20 days on germination medium. Although both the explants produced well-developed somatic embryos, only 60 - 72% of the somatic embryos of both the explants developed into plantlets in this way (Table 26). The plantlets developed up to 4 - 5 cm long with leaves and roots (Plate 11 - Fig. f).

Effect of growth regulators

The development of somatic embryogenesis depends upon the type and concentration of auxin in the induction medium. Somatic embryogenesis was never observed in the absence of exogenous growth regulators. Of the two auxins (NAA, 2,4-D) tested, 2,4-D was found to be more potent for somatic embryo induction. The comparisons of different auxin concentrations, 0.1, 0.5, 1.0, 2.0, 3.0, 4.0 and 5.0 mg/l showed little difference in response, although 2.0 mg/l 2,4-D gave the highest value for both frequency and number of embryos. The addition of cytokinin (1.0 mg/l) to the induction medium supplemented with BAP slightly enhanced the frequency of responding cultures. The evaluation of efficacy of growth regulators showed significant difference between 2,4-D and NAA. Auxin is the most important factor for the regulation of induction and development of embryos. The 2,4-D or other auxins are required for the formation of embryogenic cell clusters from single cells. This indicates that auxin is an essential factor for induction of embryogenesis. BAP shows a promotive effect on embryogenesis in each phase. Cytokinin (BAP and KN) in combination with auxin (2,4-D or NAA) yielded maximum embryo production in the solid medium. By increasing the BAP concentration, there was a significant and positive effect on somatic embryogenesis.

Effect of sucrose

Among the different sugars, sucrose was found to be favorable for somatic embryogenesis producing the highest frequency and average number of somatic embryos. In the presence of fructose, dextrose and maltose, the embryogenesis was reduced (data nor shown). The embryo induction was reduced with the increasing concentrations of sucrose. Three percent sucrose gave the highest percentage of globular stage (40.2%), heart shaped (30.0%) and torpedo shaped (15.2%) in petiole explant whereas it was globular stage (35.2%), heart shaped (28.4%) and torpedo shaped (14.5%) in leaf explant (Table 27). Sucrose at 3% (W/W) gave the best response, while at lower concentrations (< 3.0%), response was less. However, higher concentrations of sucrose (>3.0%) inhibited or decreased embryogenesis. The highest embryo yield occurs at 3% (W/W) sucrose, which was highly significant at 5% level. For sucrose, the frequency of somatic embryos increased as the concentration increased to 3% (W/W) and then decreased as concentration increased.

Effect of explants

Small variations in the frequency of embryogenesis and the number of somatic embryos per responding culture for both explants were observed. Generally, petiole exhibited a higher frequency of embryogenesis and more number of somatic embryos per responding culture than leaf. The somatic embryos transferred to germination medium showed a wide range of development responses between embryos and given explants. The explants should be trimmed in such a way to exclude leaf margin and they were placed at their adaxial or abaxial side containing the surface of the medium. Some embryos failed to develop, some grew into a callus, some proliferated into more embryos, some grew into shoots or roots and some grew both. Some embryos developed abnormal cotyledons and stopped further development. Only the embryos, which were capable of developing dicotyledonary leaves were able to grow into normal plantlets.

Effect of Media

Embryogenic callus derived from both explants produced on MS solid medium was transferred to mMS, B5 and SH media containing (2.0 mg/l) 2,4-D and 1.0 mg/l BAP for the induction and development of somatic embryos (Table 28). Somatic embryogenesis induction was higher in the MS medium followed by mMS, SH and B_5.

PHYTOCHEMICAL STUDIES

A preliminary phytochemical screening both in leaf and callus has been undertaken to identify various secondary metabolites

Centella asiatica alleged to cure different ailments were screened (leaf and callus) to examine for different bioactive compounds. The various organic solvents, benzene, chloroform, ethyl acetate, acetone, butanol, ethanol and methanol were used to extract various secondary metabolites. The extracts were tested for the presence of secondary metabolites such as alkaloids, volatile oils, steroids, triterpenes, fatty acids, emodins, flavonoids, phenolics, anthracene glycosides, saponins, tannins, carbohydrates and xanthoprotein.

In the case of benzene leaf extract, almost all the compounds except emodins, anthracene glycosides and xanthoprotein were present. Whereas in the callus extract only a few compounds such as alkaloids, volatile oils, fatty acids and saponins were present. In the case of chloroform leaf extract except volatile oils, emodins and anthracene glycosides all other metabolites were present and in callus extract except steroids, triterpenes, emodins, phenolics, tannins and xanthoprotein the other compounds were present.

Similarly in case of ethyl acetate extracts, the leaf extracts showed better results than the callus extract. The callus extract showed positive results only to volatile oils, saponins and fatty acids, whereas leaf extracts, in addition to the above (except saponins and tannins) it also showed the presence of other compounds such as, triterpenes, alkaloids, flavonoids, carbohydrates and xanthoprotein

The acetone leaf extract showed the presence of almost all the compounds except alkaloids and saponins, whereas on the other hand, the callus extract showed the presence of the compounds except alkaloids, volatile oils, emodins, anthracene, saponins and xanthoprotein.

In case of butanol of leaf extract, except alkaloids, emodins, anthracene glycosides and saponins all the other compounds were present whereas in callus except anthracene glycosides and saponins all other compounds were present.

The ethanol leaf extract showed the presence of all compounds except alkaloids, flavonoids and xanthoprotein. Callus extract showed the presence of all compounds except alkaloids.

The methanolic leaf extracts showed the presence of all compounds except alkaloids and saponins, whereas the callus extracts showed the presence of all compounds except alkaloids, volatile oils, anthracene glycosides, xanthoprotein and saponins (Table 29, 30).

Table 4. Composition of the various culture media

Constituents	Concentration (mgl^{-1})			
	MS (1962)	SH (1972)	B5 (1968)	mMS
Macro salts				
NH_4NO_3	1650	--	--	1650
KNO_3	1900	2500	2500	1900
$CaCl_2.2H_2O$	332.2	151	150	332.2
$MgSO_4.7H_2O$	370	400	250	370
KH_2PO_4	170	--	--	170
$NaH_2PO_4.H_2O$	--	300	--	--
Micro salts				
KI	0.83	0.1	0.75	0.83
H_3BO_3	6.2	5.0	3.0	6.2
$MnSO_4.4H_2O$	16.9	13.2	10.0	16.9
$ZnSO_4.4H_2O$	8.60	1.0	2.0	8.60
$Na_2MO_4.2H_2O$	0.25	0.1	0.25	0.25
$CuSO_4.5H_2O$	0.025	0.2	0.025	0.025
$CoCl_2.6H_2O$	0.025	0.1	0.025	0.025
Iron source				
$FeSO_4.7H_2O$	27.85	15.0	27.8	27.85
$Na_2ETDA.2H_2O$	37.25	20.1	37.3	37.25
Organic supplements				
Myo-inositol	100	1000	100	100
Nicotinic acid	0.50	5.0	1.0	1.0
Pyridoxine HCl	0.50	0.5	1.0	1.0
Thiamine HCl	0.10	5.0	10.8	10.8
Glycine	2.00	--	--	--

Table 5. Multiple shoot bud induction response of shoot tip and axillary node explants of *C. asiatica* to cytokinins after 20 days of culture

Cytokinins (mg/l)	Shoot tip			Axillary Node		
	Bud Break (%)	Shoot number	Shoot length (cm)	Bud Break (%)	Shoot number	Shoot length (cm)
0	0.0	0.0	0.0	0.0	0.0	0.0
BAP						
0.5	9.0±2.19^{f}	0.6±0.21^{EF}	0.10±0.03^{de}	12.0±1.09^{g}	0.8±0.17^{g}	0.14±0.02^{h}
1.0	18.3±1.05^{e}	0.8±0.17^{E}	0.12±0.02^{de}	25.0±1.41^{f}	1.2±0.18^{f}	0.32±0.03^{g}
2.0	23.0±1.09^{de}	1.2±0.22^{c}	0.68±0.03^{bc}	32.0±1.09^{e}	1.6±0.21^{e}	0.86±0.02^{e}
3.0	33.0±1.10^{c}	1.3±0.17^{b}	0.92±0.03^{ab}	39.0±1.67^{d}	2.0±0.28^{de}	1.04±0.04^{de}
4.0	**41.0±1.67^{a}**	**1.9±0.03^{a}**	**1.16±0.05^{a}**	**53.0±1.09^{bc}**	**2.4±0.35^{cd}**	**1.36±0.02^{c}**
5.0	37.0±1.78^{bc}	1.5±0.42^{ab}	0.96±0.03^{ab}	48.0±1.78^{c}	2.2±0.33^{d}	1.26±0.03^{cd}
KN						
0.5	11.0±0.89^{f}	0.4±0.21^{f}	0.06±0.02^{e}	12.0±1.09^{g}	0.6±0.21^{g}	0.12±0.01^{h}
1.0	14.0±1.67^{ef}	0.6±0.21^{ef}	0.08±0.02^{de}	22.0±1.10^{fg}	0.8±0.26^{g}	0.18±0.03^{gh}
2.0	24.0±1.67^{d}	1.2±0.18^{cd}	0.32±0.03^{cd}	32.0±1.09^{e}	1.4±0.22^{ef}	0.50±0.02^{fg}
3.0	30.0±1.41^{cd}	1.6±0.21^{bc}	0.44±0.02^{c}	35.0±1.41^{de}	2.0±0.28^{de}	0.62±0.03^{f}
4.0	37.0±1.00^{bc}	1.1±0.34^{d}	0.76±0.02^{bc}	38.0±2.28^{de}	2.4±0.21^{cd}	0.98±0.03^{de}
5.0	**43.0±1.09^{ab}**	**1.8±0.17^{b}**	**0.86±0.02^{b}**	**46.0±1.67^{cd}**	**2.4±0.21^{cd}**	**1.28±0.03^{cd}**
6.0	41.0±1.67^{ab}	1.6±0.21^{bc}	0.74±0.02^{bc}	44.0±1.67^{cd}	2.2±0.17^{d}	1.14±0.02^{d}
BAP+KN						
4.0 + 4.0	36.0±1.67^{bc}	0.8±0.33^{e}	0.14±0.02^{de}	55.0±1.41^{b}	2.0±0.28^{de}	1.48±0.03^{bc}
4.0 + 5.0	**46.0±1.67^{ab}**	**2.2±0.28^{de}**	**1.64±0.02^{d}**	**62.0±1.10^{a}**	**3.4±0.28^{a}**	**1.92±0.03^{a}**
4.0 + 6.0	33.0±1.09^{c}	0.8±0.17^{e}	0.12±0.03^{de}	57.0±1.10^{ab}	3.0±0.28^{b}	1.76±0.02^{ab}
5.0 + 4.0	33.0±1.09^{c}	0.8±0.17^{e}	0.16±0.02^{de}	53.0±1.09^{bc}	2.0±0.33^{de}	1.58±0.03^{b}
5.0 + 5.0	40.0±1.41^{b}	1.2±0.18^{cd}	0.24±0.02^{d}	58.0±1.10^{ab}	2.6±0.66^{c}	1.84±0.04^{ab}
5.0 + 6.0	33.0±1.09^{c}	1.0±0.28^{de}	0.18±0.03^{de}	54.0±1.67^{bc}	2.0±0.40^{de}	1.52±0.03^{bc}

Note: Mean ± SE [cultured on MS medium supplemented with 3% sucrose] with the same superscript are not significantly different at the 5% probability level according to DMRT. Data of 25 replicates and repeated five times.

Table 6. Multiple shoot bud induction response of shoot tip and axillary node explants of *C. asiatica* to auxins in combinations with cytokinins after 20 days of culture

Auxins (mg/l)	Shoot tip			Axillary node		
	Bud Break (%)	Shoot number	Shoot length (cm)	Bud Break (%)	Shoot number	Shoot length (cm)
0	0.0	0.0	0.0	0.0	0.0	0.0
NAA						
0.1	45.0±1.41^{bc}	3.6±0.35^{bc}	3.22±0.03^{c}	55.0±1.41^{cd}	5.0±0.28^{b}	4.20±0.20^{d}
0.5	**60.0±1.67^{a}**	**4.4±0.21^{a}**	**3.70±0.02^{a}**	**73.0±1.10^{a}**	**5.6±0.22^{a}**	**4.92±0.02^{a}**
1.0	59.0±1.41^{ab}	4.2±0.17^{ab}	3.42±0.03^{b}	66.0±1.67^{b}	4.6±0.35^{c}	4.60±0.04^{b}
IBA						
0.1	40.0±1.41^{c}	3.2±0.18^{c}	3.08±0.03cd	49.0±1.67^{d}	4.2±0.33^{d}	4.02±0.03^{e}
0.5	**55.0±1.41^{ab}**	3.8±0.34^{b}	**3.20±0.04^{cd}**	**61.0±1.67^{bc}**	**4.4±0.22^{cd}**	**4.38±0.05^{c}**
1.0	50.0±1.41^{b}	3.6±0.35^{bc}	3.10±0.02^{cd}	59.0±0.89^{c}	4.0±0.40^{de}	4.08±0.03^{de}
IAA						
0.1	38.0±1.78^{c}	3.4±0.16^{c}	2.98±0.03^{d}	46.0±0.89^{d}	4.2±0.11^{d}	3.94±0.02^{e}
0.5	**39.0±2.19^{c}**	**3.6±0.16^{bc}**	**3.04±0.04^{cd}**	**56.0±0.89^{cd}**	**4.1±0.26^{de}**	**3.90±0.04^{e}**
1.0	37.0±1.09^{c}	3.3±0.19^{c}	3.00±0.02^{cd}	49.0±1.67^{d}	3.6±0.26^{e}	3.88±0.03^{e}

Note: Mean ± SE [cultured on MS + BA (4.0 mg/l) + KN (5.0 mg/l) + 3% sucrose medium for shoot tip and axillary node explants] with the same superscript are not significantly different at the 5% probability level according to DMRT. Data of 25 replicates and repeated five times.

Table 7. Multiple shoot bud induction response of shoot tip and axillary node explants of *C. asiatica* to adenine sulphate (Ads) and gibberellic acid (GA_3) in combinations with cytokinins and auxins after 45 days of culture

Additives (mg/l)	Shoot tip			Axillary node		
	Bud Break (%)	Shoot number	Shoot length (cm)	Bud Break (%)	Shoot number	Shoot length (cm)
0	0.0	0.0	0.0	0.0	0.0	0.0
Ads						
5	65.0±1.22^{f}	5.9±0.29^{f}	3.18±0.03^{e}	73.5±1.34^{cd}	6.2±0.17^{g}	4.76±0.05^{f}
10	**67.0±0.84^{e}**	**6.4±0.21^{e}**	**3.30±0.04^{e}**	**76.5±0.55^{bc}**	**6.8±0.18^{f}**	**4.96±0.02^{e}**
15	63.0±0.84^{g}	6.6±0.21^{de}	3.98±0.03^{d}	72.0±0.83^{d}	6.6±0.21^{fg}	4.92±0.03^{ef}
GA_3						
0.1	71.0±0.83^{cd}	6.8±0.28^{cd}	4.04±0.05^{cd}	74.0±1.14^{cd}	7.4±0.22^{de}	5.36±0.04^{c}
0.5	**72.0±0.54^{d}**	**7.0±0.33^{d}**	**4.12±0.02^{d}**	**78.0±0.83^{bc}**	**7.6±0.21^{d}**	**5.54±0.02^{bc}**
1.0	70.0±1.58^{de}	6.4±0.21^{e}	3.92±0.03^{de}	75.0±0.71^{c}	7.2±0.33^{e}	5.12±0.05^{de}
Ads+GA_3						
10 + 0.1	73.5±1.34^{e}	7.2±0.17^{c}	4.40±0.04^{b}	74.5±1.48^{cd}	7.6±0.21^{d}	5.56±0.03^{b}
10 + 0.5	**78.0±0.54^{c}**	**8.6±0.33^{c}**	**4.92±0.04^{b}**	**83.0±1.48^{a}**	**9.2±0.33^{a}**	**5.88±0.03^{a}**
10 + 1.0	75.0±1.58^{de}	7.6±0.22^{de}	4.68±0.05^{cd}	79.0±1.51^{b}	8.8±0.33^{b}	5.60±0.04^{b}
15 + 0.1	75.0±0.83^{a}	6.6±0.21^{a}	4.32±0.03^{a}	81.0±0.55^{ab}	8.2±0.17^{c}	5.20±0.04^{d}
15 + 0.5	74.5±0.83^{b}	6.4±0.33^{b}	4.28±0.03^{ab}	77.0±0.83^{bc}	8.2±0.33^{c}	5.18±0.03^{d}
15 + 1.0	72.0±0.83^{cd}	6.2±0.18^{de}	4.18±0.03^{c}	73.0±0.83^{cd}	7.0±0.28^{ef}	5.05±0.02^{de}

Note: Mean ± SE [cultured on MS + BA (4.0 mg/l) + KN (5.0 mg/l) + NAA (0.5 mg/l) + 3% sucrose medium for shoot tip and axillary node explants] with the same superscript are not significantly different at the 5% probability level according to DMRT. Data of 25 replicates and repeated five times.

Table 8. Multiple shoot bud induction response of shoot tip and axillary node explants of *C. asiatica* to complex extracts (coconut milk-CM; casein hydrolasate-CH) in combination with the optimized concentrations of cytokinins, auxins, Ads and GA_3 after 45 days of culture

Complex Extracts (%)	Shoot tip			Axillry node		
	Bud Break (%)	Shoot number	Shoot length (cm)	Bud Break (%)	Shoot number	Shoot length (cm)
CM						
5	82.8 ± 0.17^{bc}	12.8 ± 0.33^{c}	5.56 ± 0.03^{bc}	87.8 ± 0.17^{b}	17.2 ± 0.33^{b}	6.30 ± 0.02^{b}
10	$\mathbf{85.4\pm0.22^{a}}$	$\mathbf{14.6\pm0.21^{a}}$	$\mathbf{5.92\pm0.03^{a}}$	$\mathbf{89.6\pm0.21^{a}}$	$\mathbf{18.8\pm0.17^{a}}$	$\mathbf{6.62\pm0.03^{a}}$
15	83.4 ± 0.22^{b}	13.6 ± 0.22^{b}	5.68 ± 0.01^{b}	88.8 ± 0.17^{ab}	18.2 ± 0.18^{ab}	6.34 ± 0.02^{b}
CH						
10	81.2 ± 0.33^{c}	09.6 ± 0.21^{e}	4.94 ± 0.04^{c}	83.2 ± 0.17^{d}	13.0 ± 0.40^{e}	5.42 ± 0.03^{d}
20	81.2 ± 0.17^{c}	10.8 ± 0.33^{d}	5.12 ± 0.33^{c}	84.2 ± 0.17^{c}	13.8 ± 0.33^{de}	5.44 ± 0.02^{d}
30	$\mathbf{83.6\pm0.36^{b}}$	$\mathbf{12.8\pm0.22^{bc}}$	$\mathbf{5.56\pm0.02^{bc}}$	$\mathbf{87.8\pm0.34^{b}}$	$\mathbf{15.2\pm0.16^{c}}$	$\mathbf{5.88\pm0.01^{c}}$
40	81.2 ± 0.33^{c}	11.6 ± 0.18^{c}	5.06 ± 0.02^{c}	84.4 ± 0.36^{c}	14.4 ± 0.22^{d}	5.76 ± 0.01^{bc}

Note: Mean ± SE [cultured on MS + BA (4.0 mg/l) + KN (5.0 mg/l) + NAA (0.5 mg/l) + Ads (10.0 mg/l) + GA_3 (0.5 mg/l) + 3% sucrose medium for shoot tip and axillary node explants] with the same superscript are not significantly different at the 5% probability level according to DMRT. Data of 25 replicates and repeated five times.

Table 9. Multiple shoot bud induction response of shoot tip and axillary node explants of *C. asiatica* to in combinations with the optimized concentrations of cytokinins, auxins, Ads and GA_3 and complex extracts after 45 days of culture.

Sucrose (mg/l)	Shoot tip			Axillry node		
	Bud Break (%)	Shoot number	Shoot length (cm)	Bud Break (%)	Shoot number	Shoot length (cm)
0	24.0±0.89^{c}	02.2±0.33^{c}	0.54±0.02^{c}	36.0±2.19^{c}	04.4±0.22^{c}	1.12±0.05^{d}
1	44.0±1.67^{b}	04.8±0.18^{c}	1.56±0.02^{c}	51.0±0.89b	08.0±0.40^{c}	2.38±0.03^{c}
2	72.0±1.09^{bc}	10.6±0.22^{bc}	3.12±0.03^{b}	81.0±0.89^{ab}	14.2±0.18^{b}	4.52±0.01^{b}
3	**85.0±2.00^{a}**	**14.6±0.21^{a}**	**5.92±0.03^{a}**	**92.0±1.09^{a}**	**19.8±0.17^{a}**	**6.62±0.03^{a}**
4	73.0±1.10^{bc}	11.0±0.40^{b}	3.32±0.05^{b}	84.0±1.67^{ab}	14.8±0.52^{b}	4.58±0.01^{b}

Note: Mean ± SE [cultured on MS + BA (4.0 mg/l) + KN (5.0 mg/l) + NAA (0.5 mg/l) + Ads (10.0 mg/l) + GA_3 (0.5 mg/l) + coconut milk (10.0 mg/l) medium for shoot tip and axillary node explants] with the same superscript are not significantly different at the 5% probability level according to DMRT. Data of 25 replicates and repeated five times.

Table 10. Multiple shoot bud induction response of axillary node explants of *C. asiatica* to various seasons after 45 days of culture.

Seasons	Bud break (%)	Shoot number	Shoot length (cm)
Jan	54.0 ± 1.67^{cd}	10.6 ± 0.22^{e}	5.00 ± 0.02^{c}
Feb	47.6 ± 2.28^{d}	8.2 ± 0.18^{ef}	4.48 ± 0.06^{cd}
Mar	44.0 ± 0.89^{de}	7.8 ± 0.33^{f}	3.52 ± 0.03^{d}
Apr	16.0 ± 16.7^{f}	4.2 ± 0.18^{g}	2.22 ± 0.05^{de}
May	15.0 ± 2.00^{f}	3.4 ± 0.21^{g}	2.01 ± 0.02+e
June	32.0 ± 1.09^{e}	5.4 ± 0.21^{fg}	3.12 ± 0.05^{de}
July	58.0 ± 2.28^{cd}	13.8 ± 0.17^{d}	5.24 ± 0.02^{bc}
Aug	62.0 ± 1.09^{c}	15.6 ± 0.21^{cd}	6.00 ± 0.05^{b}
Sep	79.0 ± 1.67^{b}	21.4 ± 0.21^{bc}	6.76 ± 0.04^{ab}
Oct	87.0 ± 1.10^{ab}	23.0 ± 0.49^{b}	6.96 ± 0.02^{ab}
Nov	$\mathbf{95.5 \pm 0.45^{a}}$	$\mathbf{26.6 \pm 0.21^{a}}$	$\mathbf{7.16 \pm 0.02^{a}}$
Dec	76.0 ± 1.67^{bc}	16.87 ± 0.17^{c}	6.14 ± 0.07^{b}

Note: Mean ± SE [cultured on MS + BA (4.0 mg/l) + KN (5.0 mg/l) + NAA (0.5 mg/l) + Ads (10.0 mg/l) + GA_3 (0.5 mg/l) + coconut milk (10.0 mg/l) + 3% sucrose medium for shoot tip and axillary node explants] with the same superscript are not significantly different at the 5% probability level according to DMRT. Data of 25 replicates and repeated five times.

Table 11. Multiple shoot bud induction response of different mature explants *C. asiatica* after 45 days of culture

Explants type	Bud break (%)	Shoot number	Shoot length (cm)	Basal callus (%)
Shoot tip	85.0±2.00^{b}	14.6±0.21^{b}	5.92±0.03^{b}	10.4 ± 1.09^{a}
Axillary bud	**92.0±1.09^{a}**	**19.8±0.17^{a}**	**6.62±0.03^{a}**	**0.0**

Note: Mean ± SE [cultured on MS + BA (4.0 mg/l) + KN (5.0 mg/l) + NAA (0.5 mg/l) + Ads (10.0 mg/l) + GA_3 (0.5 mg/l) + coconut milk (10.0 mg/l) + 3% sucrose medium for shoot tip and axillary node explants] with the same superscript are not significantly different at the 5% probability level according to DMRT. Data of 25 replicates and repeated five times.

Table 12. Multiple shoot bud induction response of shoot tip and axillary node explants of *C. asiatica* to different media fortified with the optimized concentrations of Ads and GA_3 in combinations with cytokinins, auxins, Ads and GA_3 after 45 days of culture.

Medium	Shoot tip			Axillary node		
	Bud Break (%)	Shoot number	Shoot length (cm)	Bud Break (%)	Shoot number	Shoot length (cm)
MS	**78.8±0.33^{a}**	**8.4±0.22^{a}**	**4.88±0.03a**	**84.4±0.22^{a}**	**9.2±0.17^{a}**	**5.92±0.03^{a}**
mMS	74.2±0.33^{b}	7.8±0.33^{b}	4.32±0.01^{b}	81.6±0.50^{b}	8.8±0.17^{b}	5.16±0.02^{b}
B_5	60.8±0.33^{c}	6.6±0.35^{c}	3.96±0.01^{b}	74.8±0.18^{c}	7.8±0.33^{c}	4.88±0.04^{c}
SH	63.8±0.33^{c}	7.0±0.28^{bc}	4.10±0.03^{b}	76.6±0.22^{bc}	8.0±0.28^{bcv}	4.96±0.02^{c}

Note: Mean ± SE [cultured on MS + BA (4.0 mg/l) + KN (5.0 mg/l) + NAA (0.5 mg/l) + Ads (10.0 mg/l) + GA_3 (0.5 mg/l) + 3% sucrose medium for shoot tip and axillary node explants] with the same superscript are not significantly different at the 5% probability level according to DMRT. Data of 25 replicates and repeated five times.

Table 13. Root formation on half strength MS basal medium supplemented with different concentrations of NAA or IBA or IAA in combination with 0.5 mg/l KN and 10.0 mg/l activated charcoal (AC) after 20 days of culture

1/2MS+ Growth regulators (mg/l)	Shoot tip			Axillary Node		
	Response (%)	No. of roots	Root length (cm)	Response (%)	No. of roots	Root length (cm)
0	0.0	0.0	0.0	0.0	0.0	0.0
NAA						
0.1	23.0 ± 1.79^{ef}	6.7 ± 0.03^{d}	0.38 ± 0.03^{e}	44.0 ± 1.67^{de}	12.6 ± 0.20^{ef}	2.94 ± 0.04^{cd}
0.5	56.0 ± 1.67^{c}	7.1 ± 0.04^{cd}	0.72 ± 0.04^{de}	65.0 ± 2.00^{c}	14.7 ± 0.13^{de}	3.36 ± 0.08^{cd}
1.0	72.5 ± 1.12^{b}	12.8 ± 0.03^{a}	2.54 ± 0.03^{c}	81.0 ± 1.41^{b}	18.1 ± 0.11^{cd}	4.02 ± 0.05^{bc}
2.0	**89.0 ± 1.67^{a}**	**18.8 ± 0.03^{a}**	**4.56 ± 0.02^{a}**	**95.0 ± 1.67^{a}**	**27.6 ± 0.08^{a}**	**5.90 ± 0.02^{a}**
3.0	70.0 ± 1.41^{bc}	12.9 ± 0.04^{b}	2.78 ± 0.05^{c}	84.0 ± 1.09^{ab}	20.0 ± 0.14^{c}	4.62 ± 0.04^{b}
IBA						
0.1	14.0 ± 1.67^{f}	5.5 ± 0.03^{de}	0.30 ± 0.03^{e}	36.0 ± 1.09^{de}	10.7 ± 0.20^{ef}	1.72 ± 0.05^{e}
0.5	47.0 ± 1.79^{de}	6.3 ± 0.04^{d}	0.62 ± 0.05^{de}	57.0 ± 1.67^{cd}	13.2 ± 0.08^{e}	2.72 ± 0.04^{d}
1.0	70.0 ± 1.09^{bc}	10.6 ± 0.03^{bc}	1.34 ± 0.04^{d}	72.0 ± 1.09^{bc}	16.7 ± 0.12^{d}	3.02 ± 0.03^{cd}
2.0	**73.0 ± 1.53^{b}**	**12.8 ± 0.05^{b}**	**3.65 ± 0.02^{b}**	**86.0 ± 0.89^{ab}**	**23.7 ± 0.09^{b}**	**4.58 ± 0.03^{b}**
3.0	68.0 ± 1.09^{bc}	9.2 ± 0.06^{c}	2.64 ± 0.05^{c}	84.0 ± 1.67^{ab}	18.2 ± 0.07^{cd}	3.98 ± 0.04^{bc}
IAA						
0.1	0.0	0.0	0.0	0.0	0.0	0.0
0.5	BC	BC	0.0	BC	BC	BC
1.0	23.0 ± 1.79^{ef}	3.3 ± 0.06^{e}	0.72 ± 0.04^{de}	26.0 ± 1.09^{e}	4.6 ± 0.01^{g}	1.00 ± 0.06^{f}
2.0	**42.0 ± 1.09^{d}**	**5.5 ± 0.03^{de}**	**2.71 ± 0.05^{c}**	**57.0 ± 1.41^{cd}**	**8.8 ± 0.15^{f}**	**3.64 ± 0.04^{c}**
3.0	30.0 ± 1.53^{e}	3.4 ± 0.04^{e}	1.34 ± 0.04^{d}	47.0 ± 1.67^{d}	7.8 ± 0.05^{fg}	2.88 ± 0.03^{cd}

Note: Mean ± SE with the same superscript are not significantly different at the 5% probability level according to DMRT. Data of 25 replicates and repeated five times.

BC - Basal Callus
0.0 - No response

Table 14. Callus induction (%) in *C. asiatica* grown on MS + 1.0 mg/l BAP fortified with various auxins after 15 days

MS basal medium + growth regulators (mg/l)	Callus induction (%)				
	Internode	Petiole	Leaf	Seed	Node
MS medium	0.0	0.0	0.0	0.0	0.0
2,4-D	78.0 ± 2.45^{de}	70.0 ± 2.45^{cd}	67.0 ± 1.09^{d}	65.0 ± 2.00^{cd}	62.0 ± 1.09^{cd}
0.1	86.0 ± 2.00^{c}	73.0 ± 1.79^{cd}	71.0 ± 1.67^{cd}	70.0 ± 1.67^{c}	65.0 ± 2.00^{cd}
0.5	92.0 ± 1.04^{b}	85.0 ± 2.00^{b}	80.0 ± 1.41^{b}	79.0 ± 1.89^{b}	74.0 ± 1.67^{bc}
1.0	$\mathbf{100.0\pm0.00^{a}}$	$\mathbf{100.0\pm0.00^{a}}$	$\mathbf{100.0\pm0.00^{a}}$	$\mathbf{93.0\pm1.09^{a}}$	$\mathbf{86.0\pm2.19^{a}}$
2.0	80.0 ± 1.41^{d}	75.0 ± 1.78^{e}	80.0 ± 1.41^{b}	80.0 ± 1.41^{b}	76.0 ± 1.07^{b}
3.0					
NAA					
	63.0 ± 1.09^{fg}	59.0 ± 1.67^{ef}	55.0 ± 1.41^{e}	42.0 ± 1.09^{f}	38.0 ± 1.09^{g}
0.1	70.0 ± 2.00^{ef}	66.0 ± 1.67^{de}	61.0 ± 0.90^{de}	54.0 ± 2.19^{e}	49.0 ± 0.90^{e}
0.5	80.0 ± 1.41^{d}	73.0±1.09c^{d}	69.0 ± 1.67^{cd}	61.0 ± 1.67^{de}	55.0 ± 1.41^{de}
1.0	$\mathbf{88.0\pm1.09^{bc}}$	**80.0±1.41b^{c}**	$\mathbf{76.0\pm1.67^{bc}}$	$\mathbf{67.0\pm1.04^{cd}}$	$\mathbf{65.0\pm1.41^{cd}}$
2.0	81.0 ± 0.90^{cd}	66.0 ± 1.67^{de}	65.0 ± 1.41^{d}	57.0 ± 1.78^{de}	54.0 ± 2.19^{de}
3.0					
IBA					
	62.0 ± 1.00^{fg}	57.0 ± 1.00^{ef}	55.0 ± 1.58^{e}	49.0 ± 0.90^{ef}	42.0 ± 1.09^{f}
0.1	70.0 ± 1.58^{ef}	63.0 ± 0.84^{de}	62.0 ± 1.00^{de}	55.0 ± 1.41^{e}	54.0 ± 2.19^{de}
0.5	76.0 ± 1.14^{de}	71.0 ± 1.14^{cd}	66.0 ± 2.07^{d}	65.0 ± 1.41^{cd}	61.0 ± 1.67^{cd}
1.0	81.0 ± 1.14^{cd}	$\mathbf{76.0\pm1.14^{c}}$	$\mathbf{74.0\pm1.14^{c}}$	$\mathbf{71.0\pm2.19^{c}}$	$\mathbf{67.0\pm1.09^{c}}$
2.0	70.0 ± 1.58^{ef}	68.0 ± 1.30^{d}	63.0 ± 0.84^{de}	63.0 ± 1.78^{d}	57.0 ± 1.78^{d}
3.0					
IAA					
	59.0±1.67g	55.0 ± 1.41^{f}	54.0 ± 2.19^{e}	42.0 ± 1.09^{f}	38.0 ± 1.41^{g}
0.1	62.0±1.09fg	61.0 ± 1.67^{e}	61.0 ± 1.67^{de}	54.0 ± 2.19^{e}	49.0 ± 0.09^{e}
0.5	66.0±1.67f	63.0 ± 1.78^{de}	63.0 ± 1.78^{de}	61.0 ± 1.67^{de}	55.0 ± 1.41^{de}
1.0	**73.0±1.09e**	$\mathbf{71.0\pm2.19^{cd}}$	$\mathbf{66.0\pm1.67^{d}}$	$\mathbf{65.0\pm1.41^{cd}}$	$\mathbf{61.0\pm1.67^{cd}}$
2.0	66.0±1.67f	62.0 ± 1.67^{de}	61.0 ± 1.67^{de}	54.0 ± 2.19^{e}	49.0 ± 0.90^{e}
3.0					

Note: Mean ± SE [cultured on MS medium supplemented with 3% sucrose] with the same superscript are not significantly different at the 5% probability level according to DMRT. Data of 25 replicates and repeated five times.

Table 15. Shoot bud differentiation (%) in *C. asiatica*, grown on MS medium fortified with various growth regulators after 20 days of culture

MS medium + growth regulators (mg/l)		Shoot bud differentiation (percent Mean ± SE)				
		Internode	Petiole	Leaf	Seed	Node
0		0.0	0.0	0.0	0.0	0.0
BAP	NAA					
0.1	0.5	76.0±1.67^{cd}	73.0±1.09^{c}	71.0±2.19^{cd}	67.0±1.09^{cd}	65.0±1.41^{cd}
0.5	0.5	80.0±1.41^{cd}	76.0±1.67^{bc}	73.0±1.09^{c}	73.0±1.67^{c}	66.0±1.67^{c}
1.0	0.5	88.0±1.09^{bc}	80.0±1.78^{b}	80.0±1.41^{bc}	73.0±1.67^{c}	73.0±1.67^{b}
2.0	**0.5**	**100.0±0.0^{a}**	**100.0±0.0^{a}**	**100.0±0.0^{a}**	**88.0±1.09^{a}**	**81.0±0.40^{a}**
3.0	0.5	81.0±0.90^{c}	80.0±1.41^{b}	81.0±0.90^{b}	80.0±1.41^{b}	70.0±2.00^{bc}
BAP	2,4-D					
0.1	0.5	69.0±1.67^{de}	61.0±1.61^{d}	59.0±1.67^{ef}	49.0±0.90^{ef}	45.0±1.67^{ef}
0.5	0.5	72.0±1.09^{d}	67.0±1.09^{cd}	62.0±1.09^{de}	54.0±2.19^{e}	51.0±0.09^{e}
1.0	0.5	80.0±1.41^{cd}	70.0±2.00^{cd}	67.0±1.09^{d}	65.0±1.41^{d}	59.0±1.67^{d}
2.0	**0.5**	**90.0±1.41^{b}**	**80.0±1.41^{b}**	**71.0±2.19^{cd}**	**69.0±2.00^{cd}**	**63.0±1.78^{cd}**
3.0	0.5	81.0±1.67^{c}	70.0±2.00^{cd}	65.0±1.41^{de}	52.0±1.41^{ef}	49.0±0.90^{ef}
BAP	IBA					
0.1	0.5	57.0±1.78^{f}	54.0±2.19^{e}	42.0±1.09^{g}	39.0±1.09^{f}	38.0±1.67^{fg}
0.5	0.5	64.0±1.67^{ef}	61.0±1.67^{d}	49.0±0.90^{fg}	49.0±0.09^{ef}	39.0±1.09^{fg}
1.0	0.5	69.0±1.67^{de}	67.0±1.09^{cd}	55.0±1.41^{ef}	59.0±1.41^{de}	49.0±1.67^{ef}
2.0	**0.5**	**72.0±1.09^{d}**	**70.0±2.00^{cd}**	**65.0±1.41^{de}**	**61.0±1.67^{de}**	**59.0±2.00^{d}**
3.0	0.5	65.0±2.00^{e}	57.0±1.78^{de}	55.0±1.41^{ef}	50.0±0.09^{ef}	50.0±2.00^{ef}
BAP	IAA					
0.1	0.5	44.0±1.67^{g}	42.0±1.09^{f}	40.0±0.90^{g}	38.0±1.09^{f}	30.0±1.09^{h}
0.5	0.5	57.0±1.78^{f}	54.0±2.19^{e}	49.0±1.67^{fg}	42.0±1.09^{f}	36.0±1.09^{g}
1.0	0.5	64.0±1.67^{ef}	61.0±1.67^{d}	52.0±1.41^{f}	50.0±2.19^{ef}	42.0±0.90^{fg}
2.0	**0.5**	**72.0±1.09^{d}**	**67.0±1.09^{cd}**	**60.0±1.41^{e}**	**59.0±1.67^{de}**	**55.0±1.67^{de}**
3.0	0.5	57.0±1.78^{f}	54.0±2.19^{e}	49.0±0.09^{fg}	49.0±1.67^{ef}	44.0±2.10^{f}

Note: Mean ± SE [cultured on MS medium supplemented with 3% sucrose] with the same superscript are not significantly different at the 5% probability level according to DMRT. Data of 25 replicates and repeated five times.

Table 16. Shoots recovered per culture in *Centella asiatica* grown on MS + 0.5 mg/l NAA supplemented with 2ip and BAP after 20 days of culture

MS medium + NAA (0.5 mg/l) + growth regulators (mg/l)	Mean number of shoots recovered/explant ±SE				
	Internode	**Petiole**	**Leaf**	**Seed**	**Node**
0	0.0	0.0	0.0	0.0	0.0
2ip					
0.5	22.3±0.06^{cd}	18.0±0.03^{de}	16.6±0.03^{e}	14.0±0.04^{d}	13.5±0.06^{c}
1.0	27.9±0.09^{c}	22.9±0.07^{de}	18.0±0.03^{de}	15.5±0.05^{bc}	15.5±0.05^{bc}
2.0	40.0±0.07^{bc}	33.3±0.11^{c}	22.4±0.04^{d}	17.9±0.05^{c}	16.2±0.04^{bc}
3.0	**59.0±0.05^{a}**	**49.0±0.04^{a}**	**40.0±0.05^{a}**	**32.3±0.04^{a}**	**24.0±0.04^{a}**
4.0	43.0±0.07^{b}	38.4±0.14^{bc}	32.3±0.04^{bc}	24.0±0.04^{b}	17.9±0.05^{b}
BAP					
0.5	15.9±0.16^{d}	13.5±0.06^{e}	12.2±0.04^{e}	8.3 ±0.04^{e}	06.1±0.14^{d}
1.0	24.1±0.04^{cd}	19.4±0.12^{de}	15.6±0.05^{e}	11.4±0.06^{de}	08.3±0.19^{d}
2.0	27.9±0.09^{c}	24.0±0.04^{d}	19.4±0.12^{de}	14.0±0.04^{d}	12.2±0.04^{cd}
3.0	**43.5±0.07^{b}**	**40.5±0.05^{b}**	**33.3±0.11^{b}**	**22.4±0.04^{bc}**	**21.8±0.09^{ab}**
4.0	40.5±0.07^{bc}	32.3±0.04^{c}	27.9±0.09^{c}	18.0±0.03^{c}	14.8±0.03^{bc}

Note: Mean ± SE [cultured on MS medium supplemented with 3% sucrose] with the same superscript are not significantly different at the 5% probability level according to DMRT. Data of 25 replicates and repeated five times.

Table 17. Root formation in *C. asiatica*, grown on 1/2 MS + 0.5 mg/l KN + 10 mg/l AC medium supplemented with NAA and IBA after 15 days of culture

1/2 MS medium + growth regulators (mg/l)	Percentage of shoots responded for rooting/ culture (Mean ± SE)				
	Internode	Petiole	Leaf	Seed	Node
0	0.0	0.0	0.0	0.0	0.0
NAA					
0.1	$65.0±2.00^{cd}$	$57.0±1.78^{d}$	$47.0±1.09^{de}$	$44.0±1.67^{de}$	$36.0±1.67^{de}$
0.5	$69.0±1.67^{cd}$	$65.0±1.67^{cd}$	$55.0±1.67^{d}$	$50.5±1.41^{d}$	$40.0±0.89^{d}$
1.0	$84.0±0.89^{a}$	$74.0±0.89^{bc}$	$70.0±1.67^{bc}$	$60.0±0.89^{c}$	$57.0±1.78^{bc}$
2.0	**$95.0±1.09^{b}$**	**$90.0±1.41^{a}$**	**$86.0±0.89^{a}$**	**$80.0±1.09^{a}$**	**$72.0±1.67^{a}$**
3.0	$70.0±1.67^{cd}$	$70.0±1.67^{c}$	$65.0±2.00^{c}$	$60.0±1.67^{c}$	$60.0±1.09^{b}$
IBA					
0.1	$64.0±1.67^{d}$	$55.0+1.67^{d}$	$44.0±1.67^{e}$	$38.0±2.00^{e}$	$30.0±1.09^{e}$
0.5	$68.0±1.41^{cd}$	$60.0±0.89^{d}$	$49.0±0.89^{de}$	$45.0±1.09^{de}$	$40.0±0.89^{d}$
1.0	$72.0±1.09^{c}$	$68.0±2.00^{cd}$	$65.0±2.00^{c}$	$58.0±1.41^{cd}$	$55.0±1.67^{bc}$
2.0	**$84.0±0.89^{b}$**	**$80.0±0.89^{b}$**	**$76.0±1.67^{b}$**	**$70.0±1.67^{b}$**	**$65.0±2.00^{ab}$**
3.0	$65.0±2.00^{cd}$	$70.0±1.67^{c}$	$60.0±0.89^{cd}$	$55.0±1.67^{cd}$	$50.0±1.41^{c}$

Note: Mean ± SE [cultured on half strength MS medium supplemented with 3% sucrose] with the same superscript are not significantly different at the 5% probability level according to DMRT. Data of 25 replicates and repeated five times.

Table 18. Callus induction in *C. asiatica* grown on various nutrient media after 20 days of culture

MS medium + 2,4-D (2.0 mg/l) + BAP (1.0 mg/l) + various media	Callus induction (%)				
	Internode	**Petiole**	**Leaf**	**Seed**	**Node**
MS	**100.0±0.0[a]**	**100.0±0.0[a]**	**100.0±0.0[a]**	**93.0±1.09[a]**	**86.0±2.19[a]**
mMS	80.0±1.14[b]	71.0±1.30[b]	66.0±1.67[b]	55.0±1.67[b]	50.0±0.90[b]
B5	70.0±1.58[bc]	63.0±1.78[bc]	54.0±2.19[bc]	49.0±1.09[bc]	38.0±1.09[bc]
SH	40.0±1.00[c]	38.0±1.40[c]	30.0±1.04[c]	20.0±1.67[c]	15.0±1.67[c]

Note: Mean ± SE [cultured on MS medium supplemented with 3% sucrose] with the same superscript are not significantly different at the 5% probability level according to DMRT. Data of 25 replicates and repeated five times.

Table 19. Callus induction [MS + 2,4-D (2.0 mg/l) + BAP (1.0 mg/l)], shoot bud differentiation [MS + BAP (2.0 mg/l) + NAA (0.5 mg/l)], shoot multiplication [MS + 2ip (3.0 mg/l) + NAA (0.5 mg/l)] and rooting [1/2 MS + NAA (2.0 mg/l) + KN (0.5 mg/l) + AC (10.0 mg/l)] response of after 20, 40, 60, 80 days of culture respectively in different explants of *Centella asiatica*

Different explants	Callus induction in frequency (Mean ± SE)	Shoot bud regeneration frequency (Mean ± SE	Shoot multiplication No. of shoots/explant (Mean ± SE)	Root induction frequency (Mean ± SE)
Internode	**100.0±0.0[a]**	**100.0±0.0[a]**	**59.0±0.05[a]**	**95.0±1.09[a]**
Petiole	100.0±0.0[a]	100.0±0.0[a]	49.0±0.04[b]	90.0±1.41[b]
Leaf	100.0±0.0[a]	100.0±0.0[a]	40.0±0.05[c]	86.0±0.89[c]
Seed	93.0±1.09[b]	88.0±1.09[b]	32.3±0.04[d]	80.0±1.09[d]
Node	86.0±2.19[c]	81.0±0.90[c]	24.0±0.05[e]	72.0±1.67[e]

Note: Mean ± SE [cultured on MS medium supplemented with 3% sucrose] with the same superscript are not significantly different at the 5% probability level according to DMRT. Data of 25 replicates and repeated five times.

Table 20. Callus induction (%) from petiole and leaf explants of C. *asiatica* grown on MS medium supplemented with 2,4-D and NAA, after 15 days

MS medium + growth regulators (mg/l)	**Callus induction (%)**	
	Petiole	**Leaf**
0.0	0.0	0.0
2,4-D		
0.1	12.4 ± 2.6[de]	10.6 ± 1.6[de]
0.5	25.6 ± 1.8[d]	22.4 ± 1.8[d]
1.0	58.2 ± 1.6[bc]	55.2 ± 2.0[bc]
2.0	**82.5 ± 2.2[a]**	**75.8 ± 2.1[a]**
3.0	65.7 ± 1.6[b]	60.9 ± 2.4[b]
NAA		
0.1	10.8 ± 1.8[e]	8.9 ± 2.1[e]
0.5	20.4 ± 2.2[de]	18.2 ± 1.8[de]
1.0	44.2 ± 2.4[c]	40.5 ± 2.2[c]
2.0	**75.1 ± 1.6[ab]**	**70.4 ± 2.4[ab]**
3.0	60.2 ± 2.1[bc]	55.1 ± 1.8[bc]

Each value was the average of 25 replicates and repeated five times.. Mean separation-using Duncan's Multiple Range Test (DMRT), means within column with different letters are significant at the 5% level.

Table 21. Somatic embryo induction from petiole and leaf explants of *C. asiatica* grown on MS + BAP (1.0 mg/l) medium supplemented with 2,4-D and NAA, after 25 days of culture

MS medium + BAP (1.0 mg/l) + growth regulators (mg/l)	Somatic embryo induction (%)		Somatic embryos/explant	
	Petiole	Leaf	Petiole	Leaf
0	0.0	0.0	0.0	0.0
2,4-D				
0.1	0.0	0.0	0.0	0.0
0.5	35.0±1.6^{ef}	22.0±2.8^{ef}	18.0±0.9^{d}	18.1±0.5^{e}
1.0	55.0±2.4^{cd}	40.0±1.4^{d}	26.0±1.0^{cd}	20.0±1.0^{d}
2.0	70.0±2.8^{b}	55.0±2.6^{bc}	35.0±1.1^{bc}	29.0±1.2^{c}
3.0	**80.0±2.3^{a}**	**70.0±2.4^{a}**	**52.0±0.9^{a}**	**46.6±1.1^{a}**
4.0	75.0±2.8^{ab}	60.0±2.3^{b}	40.0±0.5^{b}	35.0±0.6^{b}
5.0	65.0±2.3^{bc}	50.0±2.4^{c}	30.0±0.6^{c}	25.0±0.9^{cd}
NAA				
0.1	0.0	0.0	0.0	0.0
0.5	25.0±2.1^{f}	20.0±3.2^{f}	12.0±0.5^{e}	8.0±0.9^{e}
1.0	35.0±2.6^{ef}	28.0±2.4^{e}	18.0±0.6^{d}	12.0±0.5^{e}
2.0	42.0±2.4^{de}	37.0±1.8^{de}	25.0±0.9^{cd}	20.0±1.0^{d}
3.0	**60.0±1.8^{c}**	**50.0±2.3^{c}**	**35.0±1.1^{bc}**	**28.0±1.1^{c}**
4.0	50.0±2.8^{d}	40.0±2.4^{d}	30.0±1.1^{c}	25.0±0.9^{cd}
5.0	40.0±2.4^{e}	35.0±1.8^{de}	25.0±1.2^{cd}	20.0±1.8^{d}

Each value was the average of 25 replicates and repeated five times.. Mean separation-using Duncan's Multiple Range Test (DMRT), means within column with different letters are significant at the 5% level.

Table 22. Somatic embryo maturation in *C. asiatica* grown on MS + NAA (0.5 mg/l) medium supplemented with KN, after 20 days of culture.

MS + 0.5 mg/l NAA + KN (mg/l)	No. of calli plated		No. of calli showing mature embryos		Embryo maturation response (%)	
	Petiole	Leaf	Petiole	Leaf	Petiole	Leaf
0	50.0	50.0	0.0	0.0	0.0	0.0
0.5	45.0	45.0	20.0	15.0	44.4 ± 2.1^{d}	33.3 ± 2.4^{e}
1.0	45.0	45.0	25.0	20.0	55.5 ± 2.3^{c}	44.4 ± 2.2^{d}
1.5	50.0	45.0	35.0	25.0	77.7 ± 1.8^{b}	55.5 ± 2.3^{c}
2.0	**50.0**	**50.0**	**46.0**	**40.0**	$\mathbf{92.0\pm2.4^{a}}$	$\mathbf{80.0\pm1.8^{a}}$
2.5	45.0	50.0	35.0	30.0	77.7 ± 2.3^{b}	66.6 ± 1.8^{b}
3.0	50.0	45.0	35.0	20.0	70.0 ± 2.4^{bc}	44.4 ± 2.2^{d}

Each value was the average of 25 replicates and repeated five times.. Mean separation-using Duncan's Multiple Range Test (DMRT), means within column with different letters are significant at the 5% level.

Table 23. Somatic embryo germination in C. asiatica grown on MS + 0.5 mg/l NAA + 10.0 mg/l activated charcoal (AC) medium supplemented with BAP, after 15 days of culture

MS +0.5 mg/l NAA + 10 mg/l AC + BAP (mg/l)	No. of mature embryos plated		No. of embryos germinated		Conversion (%)	
	Petiole	Leaf	Petiole	Leaf	Petiole	Leaf
0	50.0	50.0	10.0	08.0	20.0 ± 1.8^{e}	16.0 ± 1.8^{e}
0.1	55.0	50.0	20.0	14.0	36.4 ± 2.2^{d}	28.0 ± 2.2^{de}
0.5	55.0	55.0	30.0	20.0	54.5 ± 2.3^{c}	36.4 ± 2.4^{d}
1.0	60.0	55.0	45.0	25.0	75.0 ± 1.8^{ab}	43.5 ± 2.4^{c}
2.0	**65.0**	**60.0**	**56.0**	**45.0**	$\mathbf{86.2\pm2.4^{a}}$	$\mathbf{35.0\pm1.8^{a}}$
3.0	65.0	55.0	45.0	30.0	69.2 ± 2.2^{b}	54.5 ± 2.2^{b}

Each value was the average of 25 replicates and repeated five times.. Mean separation-using Duncan's Multiple Range Test (DMRT), means within column with different letters are significant at the 5% level.

Table 24. Somatic embryogenesis in *C. asiatica* suspension cultures grown on MS + 1.0 mg/l BAP medium supplemented with 2,4-D after 20 days of culture

MS medium + BAP (1.0 mg/l) + 2,4-D (mg/l)	Somatic embryo induction (%)	
	Petiole	Leaf
0.0	0.0	0.0
2,4-D		
1.0	10.6 ± 1.9^{d}	8.6 ± 2.5^{e}
2.0	25.8 ± 1.6^{c}	18.4 ± 1.8^{d}
3.0	46.5 ± 2.2^{bc}	35.6 ± 1.6^{c}
4.0	$\mathbf{69.2 \pm 1.8^{a}}$	$\mathbf{60.8 \pm 2.4^{a}}$
5.0	50.4 ± 2.2^{b}	49.2 ± 2.2^{b}

Each value was the average of 25 replicates and repeated five times.. Mean separation-using Duncan's Multiple Range Test (DMRT), means within column with different letters are significant at the 5% level.

Table 25. Somatic embryo development in *C. asiatica* suspension culture grown on MS + 3.0 mg/l NAA + 1.0 mg/l KN after 10th, 20th & 30th days of culture.

Stages of somatic embryogenesis	Petiole			Leaf		
	10	20	30	10	20	30
Globular	**62.9±2.2^{a}**	40.3±2.2^{ab}	16.5±1.8^{c}	**58.6±2.2^{a}**	37.7±2.2^{ab}	15.6±1.8^{c}
Heart	29.6±1.8^{b}	**43.4±1.8^{a}**	34.2±1.6^{b}	26.9±1.8^{b}	**39.5±1.6^{a}**	33.0±2.2^{b}
Torpedo	7.4±1.6^{c}	16.3±1.6^{b}	**49.3±2.2^{a}**	6.4±1.6^{c}	14.7±1.8^{b}	**51.4±1.6^{a}**

Each value was the average of 20 - 25 replicates and repeated five times.. Mean separation-using Duncan's Multiple Range Test (DMRT), means within column with different letters are significant at the 5% level.

Table 26. Somatic embryo germination in *C. asiatica* grown on MS + 0.5 mg/l NAA medium supplemented with BAP, after 20 days of culture

MS + 0.5mg/l NAA + BAP (mg/l)	No. of mature embryos plated		No. of embryos germinated		Conversion (%)	
	Petiole	Leaf	Petiole	Leaf	Petiole	Leaf
0	25	25	3	2	12.0±1.6[d]	8.0±1.8[d]
0.1	25	25	8	6	32.0±2.2[cd]	24.0±1.9[cd]
0.5	25	25	10	7	40.0±1.8[c]	28.0±2.2[c]
1.0	25	25	13	11	52.0±1.6[bc]	44.0±2.0[bc]
2.0	**25**	**25**	**18**	**15**	**72.0±2.2[a]**	**60.0±1.9[a]**
3.0	25	25	14	12	56.0±2.2[b]	48.0±1.6[b]

Each value was the average of 25 replicates and repeated five times.. Mean separation-using Duncan's Multiple Range Test (DMRT), means within column with different letters are significant at the 5% level.

Table 27. Effect of sucrose (%) on somatic embryo development in *C. asiatica* grown on MS liquid medium + 2.0 mg/l 2,4-D + 1.0 mg/l KN after 20 days of culture

Sucrose (%)	Different stages of somatic embryos from petiole			Different stages of somatic embryos from leaf		
	Globular stage (%)	Heart shaped (%)	Torpedo Shaped (%)	Globular stage (%)	Heart shaped (%)	Torpedo Shaped (%)
0	0.0	0.0	0.0	0.0	0.0	0.0
1	20.0 ± 2.2^{bc}	10.6 ± 1.9^{c}	8.9 ± 1.8^{c}	10.4 ± 2.4^{c}	8.4 ± 2.1^{d}	6.2 ± 1.9^{c}
2	29.7 ± 1.8^{b}	20.8 ± 2.3^{b}	12.6 ± 1.8^{b}	20.9 ± 1.9^{bc}	15.4 ± 2.2^{c}	10.1 ± 1.8^{b}
3	$\mathbf{40.2 \pm 2.1^{a}}$	$\mathbf{30.0 \pm 1.9^{a}}$	$\mathbf{15.2 \pm 2.2^{a}}$	$\mathbf{35.2 \pm 2.2^{a}}$	$\mathbf{28.0 \pm 2.4^{a}}$	$\mathbf{14.5 \pm 2.4^{a}}$
4	35.0 ± 1.8^{ab}	25.0 ± 1.8^{ab}	12.4 ± 2.4^{b}	30.0 ± 1.9^{ab}	20.5 ± 1.8^{b}	10.4 ± 1.8^{b}
5	30.2 ± 0.9^{b}	20.7 ± 1.6^{b}	9.8 ± 2.1^{bc}	25.6 ± 1.8^{b}	15.4 ± 1.6^{c}	8.61 ± 2.2^{bc}
6	25.6 ± 2.1^{bc}	15.2 ± 2.2^{bc}	6.2 ± 2.1^{cd}	20.7 ± 2.4^{bc}	10.7 ± 1.8^{cd}	4.9 ± 2.1^{cd}
7	20.2 ± 2.4^{c}	10.6 ± 2.1^{c}	4.2 ± 1.8^{d}	18.7 ± 1.7^{bc}	8.4 ± 2.2^{d}	2.8 ± 2.4^{d}

Each value was the average of 25 replicates and repeated five times.. Mean separation-using Duncan's Multiple Range Test (DMRT), means within column with different letters are significant at the 5% level.

Table 28. Somatic embryo induction in *C. asiatica* grown on various nutrient media after 20 days of culture

Medium type	Globular stage (%)	Heart shape stage (%)	Torpedo stage (%)	Germination of embryo (%)
MS medium	**40.2[a]**	**30.0 [a]**	**15.2 [a]**	**10.2 [a]**
mMS	27.3[b]	20.0 [b]	10.8 [b]	2.1 [b]
B5	12.7[c]	n.d	n.d	n.d
SH	16.4 [c]	8.4 [c]	n.d	n.d

Embryo percentage denotes the number of embryos to the total number of embryos formed per flask.

Each value was the average of 25 replicates and repeated five times.. Mean separation-using Duncan's Multiple Range Test (DMRT), means within column with different letters are significant at the 5% level.

n.d. not determined due to Nil response.

Table 29. Preliminary phytochemical screening of leaf powder with various extracts of *Centella asiatica*

Name of the compound	Leaf extracts						
	Benzene	Chloroform	Ethyl acetate	Acetone	Butanol	Ethanol	Methanol
AL	+	+	+	-	-	-	-
VO	+	-	+	+	+	+	+
ST/TRI	+(TRI)	+(ST)	+(TRI)	+(TRI)	+(TRI)	+(ST)	+(ST)
FA	+	+	-	+	+	+	+
EM	-	-	-	+	-	+	+
FL	+	+	+	+	+	-	+
PH	+	+	-	+	+	+	+
AG	-	-	-	+	-	+	+
SA	+	+	+	-	-	+	-
TA	+	+	-	+	+	+	+
CHO	+	+	+	+	+	+	+
XAN	-	+	+	+	+	-	+

- Absence
+ Presence

AL - Alkaloids
VO - Volatile oils
ST - Steroids
TRI - Triterpenes
FA - Fatty acids
EM - Emodins
FL - Flavonoids
PH - Phenolics
AG - Antharacene glycosides
SA - Saponins
TA - Tannins
CHO - Carbohydrates
XAN - Xanthoprotein

Table 30. Preliminary phytochemical screening of callus powder with various extracts of *Centella asiatica*

Name of the compound	Callus extracts						
	Benzene	Chloroform	Ethyl acetate	Acetone	Butanol	Ethanol	Methanol
AL	+	+	-	-	+	-	-
VO	+	+	+	-	+	+	-
ST/TRI	-	-	-	+(TRI)	+(TRI)	+(TRI)	+(ST)
FA	+	+	+	+	+	+	+
EM	-	-	-	-	+	+	-
FL	-	+	-	+	+	+	+
PH	-	-	-	+	+	+	+
AG	-	-	-	-	-	+	-
SA	+	+	+	-	-	+	-
TA	-	-	-	+	+	+	+
CHO	-	+	-	+	+	+	+
XAN	-	-	-	-	+	+	-

\+ Presence
\- Absence

AL - Alkaloids
VO - Volatile oils
ST - Steroids
TRI - Triterpenes
FA - Fatty acids
EM - Emodins
FL - Flavonoids
PH - Phenolics
AG - Antharacene glycosides
SA - Saponins
TA - Tannins
CHO - Carbohydrates
XAN - Xanthoprotein

5. DISCUSSION

MICROPROPAGATION

Factors affecting bud break, shoot multiplication and elongation

Growth regulators

The stimulatory effect of BAP on bud break and multiple shoot formation in *C. asiatica* was similar to that reported earlier in other medicinal species including *Curcuma* spp and *Zingiber officinale* (Balachandran *et al.*, 1990), *Chlorophytum borivilianum* (Purohit *et al.*, 1994), *Piper* spp. (Bhat *et al.*, 1995), *Ocimum* spp. (Pattnaik and Chand, 1996; Sahoo *et al.*, 1997) and *Tridax procumbens* (Sahoo and Chand, 1998). Our observations of the suppression of sprouting at higher BAP (above 5.0 mg/l) concentrations were in consonance with those of Ahuja *et al.* (1982) in *Ocimum gratissimum* and *O. viride*, Pattnaik and Chand, (1996) in *O. americanum* and *O. sanctum* and more recently of Sahoo and Chand, (1998) in *Tridax procumbens.* The development of shoots with longer internodes and petioles on KN supplemented medium (Pattnaik and Debata, 1996) shows that KN was necessary for the development of healthy normal shoots (D'Silva and D'Souza, 1992). BAP and KN in the culture medium promoted the shoot sprouting frequency and multiple shoot induction. Superiority of BAP and KN in combination has been found for micorpropagation of other species also (Sharma and Padhya, 1996; Roy *et al.*, 1998; Komalavalli and Rao, 1997; Das *et al.*, 1996). Synergistic effect of a range of growth regulators in combination with cytokinin on promotion of shoot multiplication of medicinal plant species is well documented. Various successful combinations have been reported such as BAP + IAA for *Adhatoda beddomei* (Sudha and Seeni, 1994), *Alpina galango* (Anand and Hariharan, 1997), *Duboisis myoporoides* (Kukreja and Mathur, 1985) and *Veleriana wallichi* (Mathur *et al.,* 1988) and BAP + IBA for *Rheum emodi* (Lal and Ahuja, 1989) and *Gardenia jasminoides* (George *et al.*, 1993), BAP + NAA for *Gomphrena officinalis* (Mercier *et al.*, 1992), BAP + 2,4-D for *Withania somnifera* (Sen and Sharma, 1991). In the present study, NAA at low concentration (0.5 mg/l) could multiply positively the shoot when combined with cytokinins (BAP and KN) as observed in *Foeniculum vulgare* (Hunault and Du

Manoir, 1992; Du Manoir *et al*., 1985; Badoc, 1982 and *Coriandum sativum* (Kataeva and Popowich, 1993).

Additives

In the present investigation, BAP + KN + NAA + GA_3 had a noticeable synergistic influence on multiple shoot formation. The promotive effect of GA_3 in combination with BAP on shoot bud induction as well as internode elongation in culture was reported earlier in other perennial medicinal herbs including *Saussurea lapp* (Arora and Bhajwani, 1989), *Ocimum americanum, O. sanctum* and *O. basilicum* (Pattnaik and Chand, 1996; Sahoo *et al*., 1997). On the contrary, GA_3 has been shown to suppress shoot bud differentiation in *Plembago indica* (Nitsch and Nitsch, 1967) and *Dubrisia myoporoides* (Kukreja and Mathur, 1985). The preference of Ads and GA_3 for shoot bud differentiation, shoot bud conversion and elongation of buds has been well documented (Dhar and Upreti, 1999; Sahoo and Chand, 1998a, b). Thus the addition of Ads and GA_3 along with optimized cytokinins and auxins to the culture medium elicit the synergistic effect and thus bud induction was enhanced (Mohamed *et al*., 1999).

Medium

MS medium proved to be the best medium for overall growth of multiple shoots in *C.asiatica*. The use of MS medium for *in vitro* propagation has been well documented (Pattnaik and Chand 1997; 1996; Sahoo and Chand, 1998a; Dhar and Upreti, 1999). The morphogenic response of C. *asiatica* was limited by the composition of the MS vitamins. Similar results were observed in *Foeniculum vulgare* by Garcia-Rodriquez *et al*. (1978), Paupardin (1976) and Paupardin *et al*. (1980) and *Coriandrum sativum* by Kataeva and Popowich (1993). Thus the high concentration of thiamine present in B5 vitamins has been found to be one of the factors suppressing the growth and shoot bud induction of *C.asiatica*. The contrast results were observed in different culture systems (Chalupa, 1984; Barghchi, 1987). Thus the degree of growth and differentiation varied considerably with the medium constitution (Das *et al*., 1996).

Complex extracts

Coconut milk (10%) improves the quality and quantity of shoots by preventing leaf yellowing and basal callusing during multiple shoot bud induction in both the explants, in *C.asiatica*. Similar results have been reported to have promotive effect in other species (Jordan *et al*., 1985; Roy *et al*., 1998). Casein hydrolysate (irrespective of concentration) was unsatisfactory for mass propagation of *C.asiatica*. In contrast, casein hydrolysate has been reported to have promotive effect in other species (D'Silva and D'Souza, 1992, Gras and Calvo, 1996; Roy *et al*., 1998).

Sucrose

Improved growth and increase in shoot number by 3% sucrose has been demonstrated (Kataeva and Popowich, 1993) and 2% sucrose has been demonstrated (Hunault and Du Manoir, 1992). The differences in growth obtained by the alteration of sucrose concentration may reflect altered photosynthetic abilities influenced by the relative availability of sucrose in the medium and of CO_2 in the gaseous atmosphere (David *et al*., 1992), accumulation of starch in chloroplasts and soluble sugars in leaves and inhibition of ribulose bi phosphate carboxylase activity or synthesis (Capellades *et al*., 1991). Thus lesser amount of sucrose (<2%) and higher amount of sucrose (>3%) is not sufficient to support normal growth (Thomas *et al*., 1996; Du Manoir, *et al*., 1985; Hunault and Du Manoir, 1992) under shoot bud induction and shoot multiplication cultural conditions. In contrast, higher concentration of sucrose increased the number of shoots in *Anacardium occidentale* (D'Silva and D'Souza, 1992).

Seasons

Increase in response and shoot sprouting of explants during September, October and November may be due to the active growth of the plant during winter. The next best season is spring and monsoon (July and August), when plants sprout and bloom. Thus it seems that the physiological state of the plant influences the explant behavior *in vitro* (Pattnaik and Chand, 1996, 1997; Dhar and Upreti, 1999; Sahoo and Chand, 1998a, 1998b).

Explants

The slow growth of shoot tip explants when compared to axillary bud has been well documented (Ghosh and Sen 1994a; Das *et al*., 1996). The differences in growth regulator and additives requirements that exist among different nature and parts of the same plant may be attributed to the various levels of endogenous cytokinin from explants of different positions (Ghosh and Sen, 1994a; Pattnaik and Chand, 1997). As a result of these investigations it appeared feasible to achieve effective multiplication node by using defined plant growth regulators and supplements when combined with appropriate physiological state of the explant.

Subculturing of *in vitro* producing shoots

The significant differences in shoot multiplication rate obtained as a result of the plant growth regulator regimes employed during culture initiation were indicative of changing endogenous growth regulator levels and consequent differential sensitivity and requirement of the tissues for optimal shoot production during subculture (Das and Mitra, 1990; Krishnan and Seeni, 1994). Thus, the response of recultured stem node segments of shoot cultures was markedly different from that of the initial nodal explants used. Reduction of plant growth regulator composition was required to increase the shoot bud conversion frequency during repeated subcultures. Similar observations were also observed by Krishnan *et al.* (1995). Long-term micropropagation was reported, but, they did not indicate whether the regeneration rate was maintained during the time, as was maintained for 1 year by the above method (Chaturvedi *et al.*, 1984; Vaquero *et al.*, 1993).

Rooting and acclimatization and transfer of plantlets to soil

The regenerated shoots required NAA or IBA + KN + AC combination for rooting. On transfer to media supplemented with either NAA or IBA in combination with KN and AC, the growth of each isolated plantlets was enhanced with simultaneous rooting from the basal part. This is in contrast with the results of Hunault (1981, 1984) Jha and Sen (1985) Jha and Jha (1989) Patra *et al.* (1998), Banerjee *et al.* (1999), Hossain *et al.* (2000), Begum *et al.* (2000) who could observed root formation even in the absence of any cytokinin. However, they are similar to Mckently *et al.* (1991), Mroginski *et al.* (1981) and Vandemoortele *et al.* (1996) who also could not observe root formation in the absence of kinetin.

In the present study, NAA was found to be more effective for high frequency of root initiation. The highest frequency of rooting was recorded on medium containing 2.0 mg/l NAA in combination with 0.5 mg/l KN and 10.0 mg/l AC, where all shoots formed roots within 15 days of culture. The combination of IBA (1.0 mg/l), KN (0.5 mg/l) and AC (10 mg/l) was also effective for root induction (73% of shoots rooted). In contrast, observations were made by Patra *et al.* (1998), Banerjee *et al.* (1999) and Hossain *et al.* (2000), Komalavalli and Rao, (2000).

The transplantation success was about 80 - 85%. The regenerated plants of both the explants did not show any detectable variation in morphological or growth characteristic when compared with the donor plants.

ORGANOGENESIS

Recent advances in plant cell and tissue culture technology have opened up new avenues for conducting basic genetic research on higher plants at the cellular level. They have provided potentially powerful new tools in the hands of plant breeders for generating, selecting, propagating novel and medicinally important plant varieties. The results obtained on the *in vitro* culture of different explants are discussed below.

Callus initiation

The classical findings of Skoog and Miller (1957) showed that organogenesis in tissue culture is governed by the balance of auxin and cytokinin in the medium can not be demonstrated universally due to the explant sensitivity or the content of endogenous growth regulators. Methods have been developed for reproducible plant regeneration from different explants of *C.asiatica*. Results obtained from this experiment revealed that *C.asiatica* explants differed in growth regulator requirements for callus induction, shoot bud regeneration, multiple shoot formation and root initiation. In the present study, of the four-auxin combinations (2,4-D, NAA, IBA and IAA) along with 1.0 mg/l BAP tested for their callusing ability, 2,4-D (2.0 mg/l) and BAP (1.0 mg/l) combination was in general observed to be the more effective than other combinations for callus initiation. The order of effectiveness was 2,4-D>NAA>IBA>IAA. Our results indicated that the addition of cytokinin increased the frequency of callus induction.

The callus induction frequency differed among different auxins treatments. So, the present study clearly indicates that the auxin type was greatly influenced the callus induction. Of the four auxins tested, 2,4-D induced maximum frequency of callus induction (100%) followed by NAA (88%), IBA (81%) and IAA (73%) after 15 days. This is in similar with the observation made by Wakhlu and Sharma (1998) in *Heracleum candicans* and Ignacimuthu *et al.* (1999) in *Eryngium foetidum*: who reported that 2,4-D (0.5 mg/l) and BAP (0.5 mg/l); 2,4-D (1.0 mg/l) BAP (1.0 mg/l) combinations induced the highest frequency of callusing within 15 days respectively. This is in contrast with the observation made by Patra *et al.* (1998) and Banerjee *et al.* (1999) in *C.asiatica* who reported that 4.0 mg/l NAA and 2.0 mg/l KN; 0.1 mg/l IBA and 3.0 mg/l BAP combinations induced highest frequency of callusing within 15 days. In the present study, the callusing was increased with increase in the concentration of auxin supplemented with 1.0 mg/l BAP in the medium. The callus induction was increased in all the explants with four auxin combinations of five explants tested in the present study. This is considered with reports of the culture of different explants of *C.asiatica* (Patra *et al.*, 1998). However, Atreya *et al.* (1984) observed only 60% of callus induction on MS medium supplemented with 2.0 mg/l NAA alone in *Arachis hypogaea.*

In the present study, the percentage of callus induction was found to be high (100%) over previous reports. The callusing frequency was enhanced with the addition of cytokinin (BAP) in the medium. The highest frequency of callusing was observed only in the presence of BAP in the medium along with auxin. The present study, clearly showed that the cytokinin type was obviously influenced the callusing frequency. Patra *et al.* (1998) observed 80% callusing frequency on a medium with 2.0 mg/l KN and 4.0 mg/l NAA within 15 days of culture. Banerjee *et al.* (1999) reported that the combination of IBA (0.1mg/l) and BAP (2.0 mg/l) induced maximum frequency of callusing (90%) within 20 days.

In the present experiment, the maximum frequency of callusing (100%) was observed within 20 days of culture initiation. Abubacker and Alagumanian (1999) in *Azadiracta indica* obtained 100% of callusing on a medium with IAA (0.5 mg/l) and BAP (1.0 mg/l), 100% of callus induction was observed by Prem and Hailing Xu (1999) in *Scaevola phlebopetala* in the presence of BAP (1.0 mg/l), 2,4-D (0.5 mg/l) and coconut milk (5%) within 15 days of culture. Abubacker and Murugesan (1999) in *Sorghum bicolor* obtained 100% of callusing on a medium with BAP (1.5 mg/l) and NAA (0.5 mg/l) within 15 days of culture.

The callus induction was high in internode explant followed by petiole, leaf, seed and node. The highest frequency of callus formation (100%) was observed in internode, petiole and leaf explant with 2.0 mg/l 2,4-D and 1.0 mg/l BAP combination than seed (93%) and node (86%) after 15 days of culture. This is in agreement with earlier workers in *C.asiatica* (Patra *et al*., 1998; Banerjee *et al*., 1999; Hossain *et al*., 2000) but the frequency of callusing was lesser than the present experiment. The mature petiole (Wakhlu and Sharma, 1998) and leaf (80%) induced high frequency of callusing within 15 days of culture (Banerjee *et al*., 1999). Stem and leaf explants induced (100%) of callusing in *C.asiatica* (Patra *et al*., 1998; Banerjee *et al*., 1999) with various growth regulator concentrations and combinations in different durations. But in the present experiment, 2,4-D (2.0 mg/l) and BAP (1.0 mg/l) combination was found to be the superior for 100% of callusing using internode, petiole, leaf explants after 15 days of culture. Data on callus formation of the different explants of MS basal medium showed some variations. Although 1.0 or 2.0 mg/l of auxin alone gave callus, the growth was poor in comparison with auxins (2.0 mg/l) supplemented with BAP (1.0 mg/l) (Wakhlu and Sharma, 1998). Although 2,4-D is a potent auxin to stimulate callus induction, is found to be more effective in association with BAP, as their combination is essential for callus induction. The similar results were also reported in *Heracleum candicans* by Wakhlu and Sharma (1998).

The previous workers were used higher concentrations of auxins as well as cytokinin for callus induction but they observed maximum 80% after 25 days of culture. The present study had some distinct advantages over previous reports. 2.0 mg/l of auxin and 1.0 mg/l of BAP itself sufficient to induce maximum frequency of callusing in different explants. The highest frequency of callusing (100%) was observed after 15 days of culture initiation.

Shoot bud differentiation

In the present study, the shoot bud regeneration efficiency was enhanced from different mature explants derived callus by culturing them on MS basal medium containing different concentrations of BAP (0.5 - 3.0 mg/l) with low level (0.5 mg/l) of various auxins (NAA, 2,4-D, IBA and IAA). In the absence of BAP, however there was no induction of shoot bud regeneration. But shoot bud regeneration frequency increased with the increase in the concentration of BAP upto optimum level

(2.0 mg/l). Among the auxins used, the shoot bud regeneration frequency was found to be the highest in NAA followed by 2,4-D, IBA and IAA in combination with BAP. The induction of shoots by BAP in combination with auxin (NAA) is in agreement with reports of *C.asiatica* cultures (Patra *et al.*, 1998; Banerjee *et al.*, 1999; Hossain *et al.*, 2000) and other Apiaceae members like *Angelica sinensis* (Zhang and Chang, 1989) and *Carum curvi* (Krens *et al.*, 1997).

In the present investigation, 90% of shoot bud regeneration was observed on a medium containing 2.0 mg/l BAP and 0.5 mg/l NAA within 20 days of culture. This is in contrast with the observation made by Banerjee *et al.* (1999) in *C.asiatica* who reported that 60% of shoot bud regeneration on a medium containing 3.0 mg/l BAP and 0.05 mg/l NAA and the frequency of shoot bud induction was reduced by 50% when the same calli were transferred to medium with BAP (2.0 mg/l) and NAA (0.5 mg/l). Manjula *et al.* (1997) reported that BAP (2.0 mg/l) and NAA (0.5 mg/l) combination induced 80% shooting from nodal segments explants in *Aristolochia indica* within 28 days and similar combination induced 75% shoots from leaf explants of *C.asiatica* (Banerjee *et al.*, 1999). But in the present study, 2.0 mg/l BAP and 0.5 mg/l NAA induced highest frequency of shoot bud regeneration (100%) from internode, petiole and leaf explants followed by seed (88%) and node (81%) explants after 20-25 days of culture. However, an increase in BAP concentration, the shoot bud regeneration frequency was also increased considerably. Addition of BAP to the medium also reduced shoot regeneration. This is in agreement with earlier reports in *Scitrullus lanatus* (Janosi *et al.*, 1991), *Rauwolfia micrantha* (Sudha and Seeni, 1996), *Aristolochia indica* (Manjula *et al.*, 1997), *Sorghum bicolor* (Abubacker and Murugesan, 1999), *Azadirachta indica* (Abubacker and Alagumanian, 1999) and *C.asiatica* (Banerjee *et al.*, 1999; Hossain *et al.*, 2000).

In the present study, of the different calli used, internode derived callus was found to be more suitable for high frequency of shoot bud differentiation followed by petiole, leaf, seed and node explant derived calli, whereas direct shoot bud regeneration was observed from petiole explant. These variations in the regeneration potential among explants are attributable to the differences in their physiological status. Variation of shoot forming ability of calli derived from various explant sources has also been noted by Zhang and Chang (1989), Becker (1970), Hunault (1981,

1984), Krens *et al*. (1997), Patra *et al*. (1998), Arockiasamy and Ignacimuthu (1998), Banerjee *et al*. (1999) and Hossain *et al*. (2000).

Multiple shoot bud regeneration

The cytokinins (2ip and BAP) enhanced multiple shoot bud regeneration in callus of *C.asiatica.* It is in accordance with previous reports of Wang and Pierre (1995), Gupta *et al*. (1997), Lakshmanan *et al*. (1997), Ozgen *et al*. (1998), Carneiro *et al*. (1999), Mohamed *et al*. (1999) and Sivakumar and Krishnamurthy (2000).

In the present study, the highest number of multiple shoots was also observed on MS basal medium fortified with different concentrations of cytokinins 2ip or BAP (1.0 - 4.0 mg/l) in combination with 0.5 mg/l NAA. Of the two cytokinins tested, 2ip was found to be superior cytokinin for multiple shoot bud production. In the present study, it was clearly observed that 2ip (3.0 mg/l) and NAA (0.5 mg/l) were significantly effective for shoot multiplication. Angelini and Allavena (1989) reported that NAA (0.05 mg/l) and 2ip (10.0 mg/l) increased the frequency of regeneration in *Phaseolus coccineus*. This result was in contrast to the present study in which NAA (0.5 mg/l) and 2ip (3.0 mg/l) increased the frequency of the number of shoots. At the same time when >3.0 mg/l 2ip decreased shoot multiplication. Gulati and Jaiwal (1992 and 1994) reported that in *Vigna radiata*, 2ip was more effective resulting in multiple shoot induction (6.4) rather than shoot elongation but BAP showed greater response resulting in multiple shoot induction as well as shoot elongation. Zagorska and Dinitrov (1995) reported in *Medicago sativa*, 2ip (1.0 mg/l) was more effective and favoured organogenesis from leaf explant derived callus. Similar results were observed in the present study were shoot multiplication capacity was higher in *C.asiatica* cultures using cytokinins. In general, prolific shoot generation occurred in the media supplemented with a high cytokinin to auxin ratio (Ozgen *et al*., 1998; Patra *et al*., 1998). Among the several growth regulators tested, NAA in combination with BAP was the most effective where multiple shoot formation was spectacular in the internode explant of *Centella asiatica* (Patra *et al*., 1998).

The highest number of multiple shoots was observed from internode derived calli followed by petiole, leaf, seed and node derived calli. This is contrast with previous reports in *C.asiatica* by Patra *et al*. (1998), Banerjee *et al*. (1999) and Hossain *et al*. (2000). But the present experiment shows that the maximum number of multiple shoots (50 shoots/explant) was induced from internode calli after 15-20 days of culture. This is in contrast with the results reported by Banerjee *et al.* (1999) who obtained 20 shoots/explant on a medium containing 3.0 mg/l BAP and 0.05 mg/l NAA.

The enhanced effect of BAP over other cytokinins for shoot bud induction has been attributed to the abilities of plant tissues to metabolize the natural growth regulators more readily than other synthetic growth regulators or to the ability of BAP to induce endogenous production of Zeatin (Barna and Wakhlu, 1994).

Root induction

The regenerated shoots require auxins for rooting. On transfer to media supplemented with either NAA or IBA in combination with KN and AC, the growth of each isolated plantlet was enhanced with simultaneous rooting from the basal part. This is in contrast with the results of Hunault (1981, 1984), Jha and Sen (1985), Jha and Jha (1989), Patra *et al.* (1998), Banerjee *et al.* (1999), Hossain *et al.* (2000), Begum *et al.* (2000) who could observed root formation even in the absence of any cytokinin. Mckently *et al.* (1991), Mroginski *et al.* (1981) and Vandemoortele *et al.* (1996) who also could not observe root formation in the absence of kinetin.

In the present study, NAA was found to be more effective for high frequency of root initiation. The highest frequency of rooting was recorded on medium containing 2.0 mg/l NAA in combination with 0.5 mg/l KN and 10.0 mg/l AC, where all shoots formed roots after 10-15 days of culture. The combination of IBA (1.0 mg/l), KN (1.0 mg/l) and AC (10.0 mg/l) was also effective for root induction (84%).

Hardening and acclimatization of plantlets

The transplantation success was about 80 - 85%. The regenerated plants of various explants (internode, petiole, leaf, seed and node) did not show any detectable variation in morphological or growth characteristic when compared with the donor plants.

Explants

Selection of explant have a definite role in callus formation. Explants of internode have resulted in a high frequency of callus formation as compared to other explants. The results showed that the frequency of shoot bud regeneration and number of shoots per explant vary from explant to explant. The variation in callus induction, bud or shoot formation and shoot multiplication among various explants was also reported by Kerns *et al*. (1996) in *Carum carvi*, Hunault (1981, 1984) in *Foeniculum vulgare*, Patra *et al*. (1998) in *C.asiatica*. Among the different explants, internode explant was found to be more efficient for organogenesis than other explants.

SOMATIC EMBRYOGENESIS

Callus Induction

Soft, friable, whitish yellow callus is usually recommended for the induction of somatic embryogenesis in both solid and liquid cultures (Kumar *et al*., 1988; Eapen and George, 1990; Kulothungan *et al*., 1995). In the present study, the callusing response of different explants varied. Petiole explants produced maximum callus than leaf explants. This was in contradiction to the results obtained by Krens *et al*. (1997), where hypocotyls proliferated faster than cotyledonary nodes in *Carum carvi*. In the present study, the type and morphological nature of callus induction from different explants also varied. Petiole explants produced whitish yellow and friable calli, while leaf explants produced yellowish brown and less compact calli. This is in contradiction to the results of Barna and Wakhlu (1994) in *Cicer arietinum*; Manjula *et al*. (2000) in *Tylophora indica* and in *Heracleum candicans* by Wakhlu and Sharma (1998), where the petiole segments produced highly friable, whitish, shiny and watery callus, while leaf explant initiated soft, friable and nodular calli. Long time exposure of these calli on the same medium resulted in browning of tissues, which might be due to depletion of 2,4-D in the medium declining of growth. This is in corroboration with the reports of Bhojwani and Razdan (1983), Lazzeri *et al*. (1985) and Shajahan (1994).

Somatic embryo induction and development

The present study shows that the somatic embryo induction in *C.asiatica* was dependent on the type and concentration of auxin used. Somatic embryos were produced from the calli derived from both petiole and leaf explants with media containing either 2,4-D or NAA in combination with 1.0 mg/l BAP. In the present study, both auxins decreased somatic embryogenesis at higher concentrations. 2,4-D was found to be the best auxin producing the highest number of somatic embryos per culture. 2,4-D has been widely used for somatic embryogenesis in Apiaceae members like *C.asiatica* (Kim *et al.,* 1995), *Eryngium foetidum* (Ignacimuthu *et al.,* 1999), *Apium graveolens* (Toth and Lacy, 1992), *Foeniculum vulgare* (Hunault and Du Manoir, 1992; Hunault, 1981, 1984; Simard, 1985), *Dacus carota* (Halperin and Wetherell, 1964), *Heracleum candicans* (Wakhlu and Sharma, 1998) and *Angelica sinensis* (Zhang and Chang, 1989). Auxin was found to be essential for induction of somatic embryogenesis and both (NAA and 2,4-D) the tested auxins, 2,4-D was more effective in recovering mature somatic embryos. The data showed the importance of exogenous auxin in regulating *C.asiatica* somatic embryogenesis. Auxin type and concentration had specific effects on the process, both in terms of efficiency and of embryo morphology. Considering the efficiency of embryogenesis, media containing 2,4-D produced a largest number of somatic embryos compared to NAA. This finding agrees with the report of Ignacimuthu *et al.* (1999), Wakhlu and Sharma, (1998) and Hunault (1981,1984). NAA was found better than 2,4-D for induction of globular and heart shaped somatic embryos in *C.asiatica* (Kim *et al.,* 1995). Of all the evaluated concentrations, 3.0 mg/l 2,4-D and 1.0 mg/l BAP with 3% (W/V) sucrose was found to be optimum for the induction of somatic embryogenesis (80%) and maximum (52 embryos/ culture) number of somatic embryos were recorded in petiole, whereas in leaf explant produced 70% of somatic embryogenesis and (46.6 embryos/culture). Similar results were also recorded and reported in *Medicago sativa* by Kao and Michayluk (1981), *Populus deltoides* by Michler and Bauer (1991), *Arachis hypogaea* by Ramadev Reddy and Reddy (1993) and *C.asiatica* by Kim *et al.,* (1995). In contrast, addition of cytokinin to the induction medium containing 2,4-D did not enhance the average number of somatic embryos (Eapen and George, 1993a).

Somatic embryo maturation

All somatic embryos failed to undergo further development when subcultured on the same medium. Transfer of embryogenic cultures to maturation medium containing MS basal medium with different concentrations of KN (0.1 - 3.0 mg/l) in combination with NAA (0.5 mg/l) stimulated development of young embryo stages but generally repressed shoot outgrowth. Similar requirements have been observed for maturation of *C.asiatica* somatic embryogenesis (Kim *et al.*, 1995). On the maturation media calli turned green and developed into mature embryos. MS basal medium with 2.0 mg/l KN and 0.5 mg/l NAA was the best combination for maturation of embryos.

Somatic embryo germination

Of the different combinations of BAP (0.1 - 3.0 mg/l) tested, 2.0 mg/l BAP and 0.5 mg/l NAA combination was found to be the best for embryo conversion. When the concentration of BAP was increased from 0.1-2.0 mg/l, the frequency of embryo germination also increased. Further increase in the BAP above the optimum level (>2.0 mg/l) decreased embryo germination. The differentiation of somatic embryos, like that of shoots, was also induced by higher concentrations of BAP. The present investigation clearly showed that BAP was playing an important role in embryo germination. The improved response for embryogenesis in the presence of NAA and BAP combination compared to 2,4-D suggests that cytokinins are necessary for germination of somatic embryos in *C.asiatica.* Similar observations were made by Kim *et al.* (1995) in *C.asiatica.* Setterfield (1963) opined that auxins and cytokinins might act synergistically to promote both cell division and cell expansions depending upon other factors within the cell, which react with tested growth regulators. Wakhlu and Sharma (1998) also reported that embryos required an exposure to cytokinin, BAP or KN for the development of normal *Heracleum candicans* plantlets.

SOMATIC EMBRYOGENESIS IN LIQUID MEDIUM

Callus Induction

Petiole and leaf explants from 2 - 3 year-old field grown plants showed callus induction on the medium containing 2,4-D, NAA and BAP. Calli were highly variable in colour and texture. Callus was green, yellow, white and brown in colour. Some cultures were rough surfaced, friable and white, others smooth surfaced and hard. Calli, white and cream coloured and friable, were selected and subcultured.

Somatic embryo induction

In our experiments, petiole derived callus showed the highest somatic embryo formation on low concentrations of auxins such as NAA and 2,4-D in combination with 0.5mg/l BAP, compared to leaf explant. Petiole was the most responsive in producing somatic embryos in *C. asiatica* (Kim *et al.*, 1995). It is generally recognized that embryogenic callus cultures in Apiaceae are specifically obtained by culturing petiole on media containing high levels of auxin such as 2,4-D and NAA (Wakhlu and Sharma, 1998; Ignacimuthu *et al.*, 1999; Ernst *et al.*, 1984; Hunault *et al*., 1989; Hunault, 1981,1984; Simard, 1985; Hunault and Du Manoir, 1992) within 20 days. Cells were undergone for cell division and produced globular stage embryos. Development of globular embryos was observed on proliferation medium within 35 days of culture.

Somatic embryo maturation and germination

The developmental changes at more advanced stages such as heart, torpedo and dicotyledonary shaped embryos were observed on embryo maturation medium after a second subculture. Mature embryos were transferred to germination medium for plantlets development. The well-developed somatic embryos of *C.asiatica* were transferred to the medium supplemented with NAA and BAP for further development into plantlets. The development of shoot and root poles was observed within 15 days of culture. All the embryos are not undergone for germination. Only 60 - 70% of embryos were responded in this medium and shoot elongation was observed. In the present study, both auxin (NAA) and cytokinin (BAP and KN) were used for embryo germination. It clearly shows that both NAA and BAP are very essential for simultaneous development of shoot and root poles from the embryos.

Effect of growth regulators

Auxins are known to induce somatic embryogenesis in most of the plant tissue systems (Evans *et al*., 1981). Sometimes positive and sometimes negative effect of auxins and cytokinins on somatic embryogenesis, may be related to the endogenous hormone content of the explant and/or to their hormonal sensitivity (Patel *et al*., 1991). In the present study, it was feasible to use 2,4-D or NAA to obtain callus and produce regenerated plants via. somatic embryogenesis. The extent of callus proliferation on induction medium with NAA was markedly less than that on callus initiation medium with 2.4-D. Eapen and George (1993a) reported that the highest frequency of somatic embryogenesis was observed on MS medium containing 2,4-D than other auxins.

It is generally recognized that the embryogenic induction by 2,4-D is a common effect. 2,4-D has proved to be useful to obtain a somatic embryogenic response in a number of plant species from twenty dicotyledons and monocotyledons families (Ammirato, 1984). Rangasamy (1986) opined that gradual removal of 2,4-D promoted embryogenesis in most of the angiosperms. In accordance with earlier reports, in the present experiment, 2.0 mg/l 2,4-D induced embryogenic callus from leaf explants on callusing medium. The gradual reduction in the concentration of 2,4-D in the embryo development medium promoted further differentiation and development of somatic embryos. In contrast, this regulator inhibits embryo development in other species such as *Corylus avellan* (Perez *et al.*, 1986). This growth regulator was successfully used to induce the embryo formation from Apiaceae members on solid medium (Kim *et al.*, 1995; Wakhlu and Sharma, 1998; Ignacimuthu *et al.,* 1999; Hunault 1981, 1984). Ramesh and Ganapathi (1999) reported in pigeon pea that addition of IAA, NAA and IBA did not favor somatic embryogenesis but 2,4-D played a vital role. Similar results were obtained in the present study, i.e. the supplementation of IAA, NAA and IBA did not induce somatic embryogenesis but 2,4-D alone played stimulatory role in somatic embryogenesis. Addition of any one of cytokinins along with 2,4-D, improved embryo induction and development in *Vigna acontifolia*, *V.radiata* and *V.mungo* (Kumar *et al.*, 1988; Eapen George, 1990). In the present study, addition of low concentration of BAP promoted green callus formation and showed no sign of embryo induction. Similar results were also observed in cowpea (*Vigna anguiculata*), where addition of BAP to embryogenic induction medium resulted in recallusing of embryos. These results indicate that BAP reduced the efficiency of 2,4-D, as reported in peanut (Eapen and George, 1993a). Lazzeri *et al.* (1987) reported that NAA induced somatic embryo germination at higher frequencies than 2,4-D. In the present study, 2,4-D induced somatic embryogenesis but maturation and germination occurred in NAA.

In the present study it is revealed that the addition of NAA is necessary not only for embryo maturation but also for their germination. Previous reports with Apiaceae (Toth and Lacy, 1992; Zhang and Chang, 1989; Ignacimuthu *et al.*, 1999) have documented the requirement of exogenous auxin for the development of somatic embryogenesis in *in vitro*. In this study, the effect of auxin type and concentration were evaluated and found to be influence the embryo developmental process. Auxin concentrations were also significantly affected the callus induction and number of embryos. The highest frequency of embryos was (80 %) observed on a medium containing 3.0 mg/l 2,4-D or NAA.

Sucrose response

Among the different carbon sources tested for somatic embryogenesis in *C.asiatica*, sucrose evoked the best response followed by fructose, dextrose and maltose. Similar results were obtained in *V.anguiculata* (Kulothungan, 1997). The most commonly used carbohydrate for plant tissue culture is sucrose (Eapen and George, 1993a). In nature, carbohydrate is transported within plant tissues as sucrose and tissue may have an inherent capacity for uptake, transport and utilization of sucrose. Sucrose at 3% produced the best results in *C.asiatica*. Sucrose influence on somatic embryo yield and morphology in Apiaceae members (Ignacimuthu *et al*., 1999; Wakhlu and Sharma, 1998; Hunault and Du Manoir 1992; Hunault *et al*., 1984).

Effect of Media

Nutrient concentrations and their ratios in the culture medium significantly affect the induction and development of somatic embryos. Requirement of higher level of nitrogen for the induction of somatic embryogenesis was well established in several plants such as maize (Armstrong and Green, 1985), *Agrostis alba* (Shetty and Asano, 1991), *Picea mariana* (Khlifi and Tremblay, 1995) and *Beta vulgaris* (Sounders and Tasi, 1999). In the present investigation, MS medium was found to be highly suitable for the induction of embryogenic callus than mMS, B5 and SH. According to Sharp *et al*. (1980) and Eapen and George (1990), low nitrogen is sufficient for initiation and development of somatic embryos. Kulothungan (1997) reported that higher level of nitrogen in MS-B5 liquid medium supported the initiation of higher number of globular embryos than LC and B5 media. This is in contrast to the present study where higher level of nitrogen in MS basal medium supported the initiation of higher number of globular embryos than mMS, B5 and SH media.

Effect of explant

The nature of the explant has varied impact on induction and development of somatic embryogenesis regardless of the medium composition as observed in the present study. Petiole explant has proved to be better than leaf explant in somatic embryogenesis. Toth and Lacy (1992) and Wakhlu and Sharma (1998) observed significant differences among Apiaceae members for somatic embryo formation, subculture and plant regeneration. Explants remain the factor with the greatest influence of frequency of somatic embryogenesis in *C.asiatica* (Kim *et al.,* 1995) and other Apiaceae members (Hunault, 1981, 1984; Hunault and Du Manoir, 1992).

PHYTOCHEMICAL STUDIES

The production of secondary metabolites in plants is often restricted to specific tissues and organs during particular developmental stages. The morphological differentiation of plant cells into specialized cell types and tissues is accompanied by chemical differentiation that establishes the metabolic pathway leading to secondary metabolite formation. The phytohormone auxin has been proposed to act as a regulator of the switch between cell growth and secondary product formation (Goddin *et al.*, 1992; Pasquali *et al.*, 1992). Hormone composition is often a critical factor in secondary product accumulation. The type and concentration of auxin and cytokinin usually in combination have also been shown to affect cell division, cell enlargement and root or shoot differentiation.

A large number of callus and suspension cultures usually harvested after their rapid growth phase has been completed, have been examined for the presence of secondary products characteristic of the whole plant or some organs of the plant.

In general, callus tissues retain the characteristics of the plant from which they are derived in their biosynthetic and regenerative potentiality. *Vinca, Atropa* and others produced compounds of pharmaceutical interest in their tissue culture as from intact plants (Yeoman, 1986).

The potential for synthesis of chemicals by plants is enormous, ranging from highly pure compounds of pharmaceutical value to complex food materials. Growing interest in the practical aspects of plant tissue culture led to the exploration of cell culture system for the biosynthesis of a variety of natural products, a venture that has blossomed into a new technology with significant impact on plant biochemistry and industry. The production of a range of chemicals by using plant tissue culture is remarkable (Dougall, 1985).

It was recognized that different tissue explants taken from different parts of a plant within and between genotype have varying growth regulator requirements for callus growth. Callus cultures may be derived from a wide variety of plant organs or from specific cell types. The general growth characteristics of a callus involve a complex relationship among the plant material used to initiate the callus, the composition of the medium and the environmental conditions during the incubation period.

As the production of active principles *in vitro* is associated with differentiation process, differentiation experiments were undertaken to evaluate its effect on chemical changes. Callus was induced on MS medium supplemented with various concentrations and combinations of auxin and cytokinin using different explants (petiole, leaf, internode, seed and node). Effect of basal medium modifications, growth hormones and culture conditions for callus induction was studied. The present study besides producing some scientific basis of some of the ayurvedic uses of *Centella asiatica,* indicates the necessity of conducting detailed chemical and pharmacological studies on this plant.

From the present study observation it has been shown that *in vitro* derived (2 - 3 month old) callus has phytochemical activity like that of *in vivo* leaf material. The composition of medium, precursors, elicitors and growth regulators and culture conditions may influence the bioproduction of the secondary metabolities. The factors such as hormones, dark/light cycle and temperature leads to stress condition and this stress may induce the secondary compounds in culture. This result was supported by Mantell and Smith (1983). The yield of secondary metabolities may be improved by optimization of cultural conditions. Improved yield of serpentine in *Cantharanthus roseus* cell cultures were noted due to precursor feeding (Hay *et al*., 1988) and hormonal changes (Zenk, 1977). Plant cell culture and sign of development is reviewed by Dougall (1980), Withers (1978) and Withers and Street (1977).

Various factors such as growth regulators concentration, incubation in complete darkness and continuous light exposure could have induced the secondary compounds production. Similar studies were reported by Kokate (1995) that light and temperature shift could increase the alkaloid production of C. *roseus* cultures. The quinoline alkaloid content was increased 10 - 12 folds under dark condition in cultures in *Cinchona* transformed by *Agrobacterium tumefaciens* (Kokate, 1995).

The results revealed for the first time that the biosynthesis of various secondary compounds in callus cultures of *Centella asiatica* is similar to the matured leaves in *in vivo* condition. Kokate (1995) and Tabata *et al*. (1978) demonstrated that callus cultures of *Cassia tora* could produce more than 10 times of anthraquinone derivatives (6%). Similar reports was observed by Zenk *et al.* (1977) that the production of anthraquinone glycosides increased two folds by the supply of precursor O-succinyl benzoic acid in cell cultures of *Morinda citrifolia.*

Phytochemical analysis

The preliminary phytochemical studies showed, leaf and callus materials containing more or less similar secondary compounds. A wide range of phytochemicals have been detected in plant cell cultures (Kokate, 1995 and Fowler, 1983) and this has led to the possibility of some of these compounds being produced on commercial scale. The highest levels of flavonoids are found in very young tissues such as immature fruits and leaves. This is in accordance with the results obtained from different plant parts and callus cultures of the *Citrus aurantifolia* (Agarwal *et al*., 1991).

Compared to needles or bark material extracts, *Taxus* cell cultures contain much lower quantities or pigments, waxy constituents and non-polar lipids. The extraction of taxoids from callus or cell culture material is therefore much simplified (Mondher *et al*., 1996). Biotransformation of steroids and cardiac glycosides by plant cell cultures have been studied extensively and reviewed by Reinhard (1974), Alfermann *et al*. (1977), Funiya (1978) and Stohs (1977).

Similar observation was reported by Govind *et al.* (1992) who isolated the quaternary alkaloids in stems of *Magnolia acuminata.* A wide range of phytochemicals had been detected in plant cell cultures (Fowler, 1983). Biosynthesis of flavones and flavonols had been extensively studied, mainly by Hahlbrock (1977). Davies (1972) rcported tannins; Williams and Goodwin (1965) reported xanthin, steroids and terpenoids in rose tissue culture studies.

6. SUMMARY

Centella species, a multipurpose medicinal plant, bears great economic importance in pharmaceutical as well in health food products industry. Plant tissue culture techniques offer new vistas for its improvement programs. The present study was conducted in five major aspects namely, micropropagation, organogenesis, somatic embryogenesis, biochemical aspects of organogenesis and embryogenesis and phytochemical studies. The salient findings of the present investigation are summarized below.

Micropropagation:

a) Culture initiation, multiplication and elongation from shoot tip and axillary node explants were achieved on simple culture medium. The medium composition was MS + BAP (4.0 mg/l) + NAA (0.5 mg/l) + Ads (15.0 mg/l) + GA_3 (0.1mg/l) AC (20.0 mg/l) + CM (10.0 mg/l) + 3% sucrose for shoot tip explant and MS + BAP (4.0 mg/l) + KN (5.0 mg/l) + NAA (0.5 mg/l) + Ads (10.0 mg/l) + GA_3 (0.5 mg/l) + AC (20.0 mg/l) + CM (10.0 mg/l) + 3% sucrose for axillary node explant.

b) BAP in combination with KN resulted in higher propagation rate in axillary node, BAP only resulted in higher propagation rate in shoot tip explants.

c) Low concentration of NAA enhanced the number of shoots than other auxins.

d) Ads and GA_3 improved the quality of shoots by preventing leaf abscission.

e) Higher multiplication rate was obtained in MS medium followed by mMS, B5 and SH medium.

f) Activated charcoal inhibited phenolic exudation and increased the shoot number in both shoot tip and axillary node explants.

g) Coconut milk improved the quality by preventing the yellowing of leaves and quantity of shoots.

h) Three percent sucrose showed better shoot induction response than other concentrations.

i) MS medium proved to be the best salts concentrations for multiple shoot bud induction and elongations of both shoot tip and axillary node explants.

j) Maximum bud sprouting response was obtained in the month of November.

k) Axillary node explant showed best response than shoot tip explants.

l) Highest rooting response was obtained when shootlets were cultured on 1/2 MS medium supplemented with 3% sucrose + NAA (2.0 mg/l) + KN (0.5 mg/l) and AC (10.0 mg/l) for explant derived shootlets.

Organogenesis

a) Of the four-auxin combinations tested for their callusing ability, 2,4-D (2.0 mg/l) and BAP (1.0 mg/l) combination was in general observed to be more effective than other nineteen combinations.

b) The callus induction frequency was increased upto 100% with increasing the concentration of auxin upto (2.0 mg/l) further increase the decreased the callus induction.

c) Among the different explant cultured, internode explant was found to be best for highest frequency of callusing followed by petiole, leaf, seed and node explants.

d) Among the twenty combinations BAP with different auxins (2,4-D, NAA, IBA and IAA), BAP (2.0 mg/l) and NAA (0.5 mg/l) combination was found to be the effective for highest frequency of shoot bud differentiation in all the explants after 20 days of culture.

e) When BAP concentration increased upto (2.0 mg/l), the shoot bud regeneration frequency was also increased further increase (>2.0 mg/l) developed the shoot bud regeneration.

f) The highest frequency of shoot bud regeneration (100%) was observed in internode, petiole and leaf explants followed by seed (80%) and node (81%) cultures.

g) Multiple shoot was observed on a medium supplemented with 2ip or BAP (0.5-4.0 mg/l) in combination with NAA (0.5 mg/l) for all the explant cultures after 20 days.

h) The number of shoots was also increased with increase in the concentration of cytokinins upto (3.0 mg/l), further increase (.3.0 mg/l) decreases the shoots in the medium.

i) Of the two auxin combinations tested, NAA (2.0 mg/l) + KN(0.5 mg/l) and AC (10.0 mg/l) combinations was found to be the superior for highest frequency of root initiation after 15 days of culture.

j) Internode derived shoots responded well for rooting response and the rooting response was increased with the increase in the auxin concentration upto (2.0 mg/l) further increase (>2.0 mg/l) decrease the rooting response.

k) Among the different explants cultured, internode explant was found to be the best for highest frequency of callusing. Shoot bud regeneration, multiple shooting and rooting followed by petiole, leaf, seed and node explants.

Somatic embryogenesis

a) Of the two auxins tested, 2,4-D was found to be the superior for callus induction in both petiole and leaf explants.

b) Among the various concentrations of auxin (2.0 mg/l) 2,4-D or NAA in combination with BAP (1.0 mg/l) was found to be the best for embryo induction in both the petiole and leaf explants after 25 days.

c) Of the auxins concentrations of KN (2.0 mg/l) in combination with NAA (0.5 mg/l) was found to be the efficient concentrations for embryo development and maturation after 20 days of culture.

d) The combination of BAP (2.0 mg/l) + NAA(0.5 mg/l) and AC (10.0 mg/l) was found to be the effective for embryo germination after 15 days of culture.

e) 2,4-D (4.0 mg/l) and BAP (1.0 mg/l) combination induced highest frequency of embryogenic cells in suspension culture within 20 days.

f) More advanced stages of embryos namely globular, heart, torpedo and dicotyledonary were observed in suspensions culture containing NAA (4.0 mg/l) and KN (1.0 mg/l) within 30 days of culture.

g) Embryo germination was activated on a medium containing BAP (2.0 mg/l) + NAA (0.5 mg/l) and AC (10.0 mg/l) within 20 days of culture.

h) Of the two explants used, petiole was found to be better explant for somatic embryogenesis in both social and liquid culture.

i) Among the carbon sources, sucrose at 3% (w/v) was found to be optimum for maximum frequency (95%) of somatic embryogenesis.

j) The frequency and number of somatic embryos were low but conversion frequency i.e. development of plantlets was high in solid culture but embryo number was high and conversion frequency was poor in liquid culture.
k) Developmental stages of somatic embryos were almost similar to that of zygotic embryo development.

BIOCHEMICAL STUDIES

a) The morphology of organogenic and embryogenic callus was found to be entirely different. Organogenic callus was compact, nodular and tightly packed whereas embryogenic calli were neither compact nor friable.
b) The total chlorophyll was increased in organogenic calli. The carotenoid was increased in embryogenic calli.
c) Increase in total carbohydrate and starch level in embryogenic calli. Total soluble sugar was found to be increased in organogenic calli.
d) Increase in total protein and ammonia level in organogenic calli. The level of total free amino acids, proline and glutamine were found to be markedly increased in embryogenic calli.
e) There was two-fold increase in DNA and RNA contents in embryogenic calli than organogenic calli.
f) Both phenols and ascorbic acids were high in the embryogenic calli when compared to organogenic calli.
g) Both peroxidase and polyphenol oxidase were found to be increased in two fold in organogenic calli than in embryogenic calli.

PHYTOCHEMICAL STUDIES

a) The one of the main objective of the present study is to initiate the callus and to perform phytochemical investigations both in callus and leaf extracts.
b) The callus induction was achieved from various explants within 20 days of incubation on MS basal medium supplemented with various concentrations and combinations of auxins and cytokinins.
c) Very high or too low concentrations of these plant growth regulators decreased the amount of callus formation.

d) The callus extracts showed the positive results for alkaloids, volatile oils, steroids, triterpenes etc.
e) But majority of the extracts showed the presence of saponins, volatile oils, fatty acids, phenolics, tannins, carbohydrates and triterpenes.
f) The leaf extracts also showed the presence of almost all the secondary metabolites but most of extracts showed the presence of saponins, volatile oils, phenolics, triterpenes and fatty acids.
g) On comparing the results, the callus extracts proved better, since the added plant growth regulators stimulated metabolites.

All these investigations have brought into light the following aspects:

The concentration of growth regulators determined the growth of the callus and its secondary metabolite production. The presence of active principle asiaticoside in the extracts of *Centella asiatica* that is responsible for its medicinal properties.

In future the leaf as well the callus extracts could be examined using Gas Chromatography-Mass Spectrometer (GC-MS medium) for further phytochemical examination. The various secondary metabolites can be quantified or estimated.

7. REFERENCES

Abbas, S. S., Prabh, S., Singh, N., Verma, P. and Pandey, K.C. 1999. A clinical study to evaluate the antigiardial effects of *Centella asiatica* (Linn.) in man. Antiseptic, 96(1): 8 - 12.

Abubacker, M. N. and Alagumanian, S. 1999. *In vitro* organogenesis of various explants of *Azadirachta indica* A. Juss (Neem). Plant Tissue Cult., 9(2): 177 - 180.

Abubacker, M. N. and Murugesan, N. P. 1999. *In vitro* organogenesis of various explants of *Sorghum bicolor* (L.) Moench (Sweet sorghum). Plant Tissue cult., 9(2) : 173 - 176.

Agarwal, S. C., Agarwal, D. and Singh, R. H. 1999. Study on the Madhya Rasayan drug Mandukaparni (*C. asiatica*) in mental retardation. South East Asian Seminar on Herbs and Herbal Medicines, Patna. P 114 : 16 - 19, January.

Agarwal, S. S. 1981. Some CNS effects of *Hydrocotyle asiatica* L. J Res. Ayur. Siddha, 11(2): 144 - 149.

Ahmad, S., Atiq-ur-Rahman, Qadeer-ur-Din and Badar, Y. 1994. Elemental analysis of a herbal drug:Intellan A neuro-energiser. Journal of Faculty of pharmacy of Gazi University, 11(1) : 83 - 90.

Ahuja A, Verma M, Grewal S (1982) Clonal propagation of *Ocimum* species by tissue culture. Ind J Exp Bio 20: 455-458

Alfermann AW, Boy HM, Doller PC, Hagedorn W, Heins MJ and Reinhard E (1977) Biotransformation of steroids by plant tissue cultures In : Plant tissue culture and its biotechnological application (Eds.) W. Barz, E.Reinhard and M.H. Zenk , Springer-Verlag-Berlin, Newyork, pp125-141

Alfermann, A.W., Boy, H.M., Doller, P.C., Hagedorn, W., Heins, M.J. and Reinhard, E. (1997). Biotransformation of steroids by plant cell cultures, In: Plant Tissue Culture and Its Biotechnological Application (Eds.) W.Barz, E.Reinhard. and M.H.Zenk, Springer-Verlag-Berlin, New York, pp. 125-141.

Amarasingham, R. P., Bisset, N. G., Millard, A. H. and Woods, M. C. 1964. Phytochemical survey of Malaya, part III, Alkaloids and saponins. J Econ. Bot., 18 : 270 - 278.

Aminuddin, S. and Singh, B. P. 1995. Regeneration of chickpea (*Cicer arietinum* L.) through *in vitro* cultures. Plant Tiss. Cult., 5 : 59 - 63.

Ammirato PV (1984) Embyogenesis. In : D.A.Evans, W.R. Sharp and P.V. Ammirato, (Eds) Hand book of plant cell culture, Vol.1,Academic Press, London.pp.82-123.

Ammirato, P. V. 1974. The effect of abscisic acid on the development of somatic embryos from cells of caraway (*Carum carvi* L.) Bot. Gaz. 135 : 328 - 337.

Ammirato, P. V. 1983. Embryogenesis. In: Handbook of plant cell culture, techniques for propagation and breeding. (Eds) Evans, D. A., Sharp, W. R., Ammirato, P. V. and Yamada, Y. Vol. 1, Mac Millan, New York. Pp. 82 - 123.

Ammirato, P.V. (1974). The effect of abscisic acid on the development of somatic embryos from cells of caraway (*Carum carvi* L.). Bot. Gaz. 135: 328-337.

Anand PHM, Hariharan M (1997) *In vitro* multiplication of greater galangal [*Aloinia galanag* (L.) Willd]- a medicinal plant. Phytomorphology 47: 45-50

Anandarajah K and Mckersie BD (1990) Enhanced vigor of dry somatic embryos of Medicago sativa L. with increased sucrose. Plant Sci. 71: 261-266

Anbuganapathi, G. 1995. The synergetic effect of vallarai and Brahmi on learning ability of albino mice and school children. International Seminar on Recent Trends in Pharmaceutical Sciences, Ootacamund, Abstr. No. 34 : 18 - 20, February.

Angelini, R. R. and Allavena, A. 1989. Plant regeneration from immature cotyledon explant cultures of bean (*P.coccineus* L.). Plant Cell Tiss. Org. Cult., 19 : 167 - 174.

Anonymous (1951) : Peradeniya manual : Amanual of weeds of the major crops ofCeylon (Ceylon Govt. Press , Colombo), No.7.

Anonymous (1959) Floral Malesina : Taxonomic Revisions (Noordhoff- K olff N. V., Djakarta) , Ser. I, Vol 4,; Vol 5, : Ser II Vol.I .

Anonymous (1988) In: The Wealth of India. A Dictionary of Indian Raw Materials and Industrial Products. Vol 11, CSIR. pp 116-118, New Delhi, India

Anonymous , (1958) The exta Pharmacopoeia (Martindale) (The Pharmaceutical Press , London) Vol. I. 24th edn 1958 Vol.II, 23rd edn 1955.

Anonymous, 1988. In: The wealth of India: A Dictionary of Indian raw materials and Industrial products. Vol II pp 163-164, CSIR, New Delhi, India.

Anubha- Srivastava, Kumbhare, V. and Bhargava, A. 1996. Phytochemical screening of some multipurpose tree species of Jabalpur (Madhya pradesh). 19 : 31 - 34.

Anzidei, M., Viovona, L., Schiff, S. and Bennici, A. 1996. *In vitro* culture of *Foeniculum vulgare* Miller, callus characteristics in relation to morphpogenesis. Plant Cell Tiss. Org. Cult., 45 : 263 - 268.

Armstrong CL and Green CE (1985) Establishment and maintenance of friable, embryogenic maize callus and the involvement of L-proline. Planta 164: 207-224

Arockiasamy, S. and Ignacimuthu, S. 1998. Plant regeneration from mature leaves and roots of *Eryngium foetidum* L., a food flavouring agent. Curr. Sci. 75: 664-666.

Arockiasamy, S., Prakash, S. and Ignacimuthu, S. 2001. High regeneration nature of *Paspalum serobiculatum* L., an important millet crop. Curr. Sci., 80 (4):

Arora R and Bhojwani S.S. (1989). In vitro propagation and low temperature storage of *Saussurea lappa* C.B.Clarke-an endangered medicinal plant. Plant Cell Rep. 8: 44-47.

Arora R, Bhojwani SS (1989) *In vitro* propagation and low temperature storage of *Saussurea lappa* CB. Clarke-an endangered, medicinal plant. Plant Cell Rep 8: 44-47

Arrillaga, I. and Merkle, S. A. 1993. Regenerating plants from *in vitro* culture of black locust cotyledon and leaf explants. Hort. Sci., 28(9) : 942 - 945.

Arumugam S, Alagumanian S and Rao, M.V. (1997). Shoot differentiation and development from cotyledon and hypocotyls explants of *Aegle marmelos* (L.) Corr. via - organogenesis. J. Swamy Bot. Cl. 14: 108-112.

Asok, D. B. and Vaidya, B. 1997. The status and scope of Indian medicinal plants acting on CNS. Indian J. Pharmacology, 29(5) : 3340 - 3343.

Atreya, C. P., Papa Rao, J. and Subramaniam, N. C. 1984. *In vitro* plant regeneration of peanut (*Arachis hypogaea*) plantlets from embryo axes and cotyledon segments. Plant Sci.Lett., 34 : 379 - 383.

Augustine, A. C. and D'Souza, L. 1997. Somatic embryogenesis in *Gnetum ula* Brongn (*Gnetum edule*) (willd.) Blume. Plant Cell Rep., 6 : 354 - 357.

Babu, T. D. and Padikkala, J. 1993. Anticancer activity of an active principle from *Centella asiatica*. Amla Research Bulletin, 13 : 46 - 49.

Babu, T. D. and Padikkala, J. 1994. DNA fragmentation is ehrlich ascites tumour cells by extract of herbal plant *Centella asiatica* (L.) Urban. Amala Research Bulletin, 14 : 52 - 56.

Backer, H. 1970. Untersuchungen zur frage der Bildung Fluchtiger stoffwechsel produkte in callus kulturen. Biochem Physiol Pflanzen., 161 : 425 - 441.

Bajaj YPS and Dhanju MS (1979) Regeneration of plants from apical meristem tips of some legumes. Curr.Sci 48: 906-907

Bajaj YPS, Kumar P, Labana KS and Singh MM (1981) regeneration of plants from seedling explants and callus cultures of *Arachis hypogaea* (L.) Indian J Exp Biol 19 : 1026-1029

Bajaj, Y. P. S. 1986. Biotechnology in Agriculture and Forestry I. Trees I Springer-Verlag, Berlin, Heidelberg. Pp 1 - 515.

Bajaj, Y. P. S., Furmanowa, M. and Olszowska, O. 1988. Biotechnology of the micropropagation of medicinal and aromatic plants. Bajaj Y. P. S. (Ed.,) Springer-Verlag, Berlin, Heidelberg. Pp 1 - 610.

Balachandran SM, Bhat SR, Chandel KPS (1990) *In vitro* clonal multiplication of turmeric (*Curcuma* spp.) and ginger (*Zingiber officinale* Rose). Plant Cell Rep 8: 521-524

Banerjee N, Maiti M, Sen S and Dutta PC (1982) Pharmacognosy of Aegle marmelos (L.) Corr., seed-a new protein source. Acta Pharm Hung 52 : 97-101

Banerjee, N., Maiti, M., Sen, S. and Dutta, P.C. (1982). Pharmacognosy of *Aegle marmelos* (L.) Corr., Seed a new protein source. Acta Pharm Hung. 52: 97-101.

Banerjee, S., Zehra, M. and Kumar, S. 1999. *In vitro* multiplication of *Centella asiatica* , a medicinal herb from leaf explants. Curr. Sci, 76(2) : 147 - 148.

Barghchi, M. 1987. Mass clonal propagation *in vitro* of *Robinia pseudoacacia* L. (Black locust). C.V. Jaszkiseri. Plant Sci. 53 : 183 - 189.

Barna, K. S. and Wakhlu, A. K. 1994. Whole plant regeneration of *Cicer arietinum* from callus cultures via organogenesis. Plant Cell Rep., 13 : 510 - 513.

Becker, H. 1970. Undersuchungen zur Frage der Bildung fluchtiger Stoffwechselprodukte in Calluskulturen. Biochem. Physiol. Pflanzen 161: 425-441.

Begum, F, Amin, N. and Azad A. K. 2000. *In vitro* clonal propagation of Holy Basil - *Ocimum sanctum* L. Plant Tiss. Cult. 10(1) : 31- 37.

Bell, C.R. and Constance, L. 1960. Chromosome numbers in umbelliferae. Am. J. Bot. 47: 24-32.

Benjamin, B. D., Roja, P. C., Heble, M. R. and Chandha, M. S. 1987. Multiple shoot cultures of *Atropa belladonna*, effect of physico-chemical factors on growth and alkaloid formation. J. Plant Physiol., 129 : 129 - 135.

Bhakuni, D. S., Dhar, M. L., Dhawan, B. N. and Mehrotra, B. N. 1969. Screening of Indian medicinal plants for biological activity, part II. Indian J. Exp. Biol., 7 : 250 - 262.

Bhardwaj, S.K. Srivastava, K.K. (1995). Effect of a composite Indian herbal preparation. CIHP (III) on avoidance learning during endurance performance of rats. Indian J. Experimental Biol., 33(8) : 580 - 584.

Bhat SR, Chandel KPS, Malik SK (1995) Plant regeneration from various explants of cultivated *Piper* species. Plant Cell Rep 14: 395-402

Bhojwani SS and Razadan MK (1983) In: S.S.Bojwani and M.K. (Eds.) Plant tissue culture. Theory and practice Elsevier. The Netherlands,pp.43-70

Bodoc, A. 1982. Contribution a letude des phenomenes d organogenesis et de callogenese de tissue *Foeniculum vulgare* subsp. Capillaceum var. vulgare (Mill.) Thellung cultives *In vitro*, analyse des constituents de l'nuile essentielle des explants. DEA Lille Univ, France, 74 pp.

Boiteau, D., and Buzas, A., Lederer and Polonsky, J. 1949. Derivatives of *Centella asiatica* used against leprosy. Nature ., 12 : 163 - 258.

Brindha, P., Sasikala, K. and Purushoth, K. 1977. B. .M. Priliminary phytochemical studies in higher plants Ethnobotanical Research 3(1) : 84-96.

Brown, D. C. W. and Thorpe T..A. 1980. Adenosine phosphate and nicotinamide adenine dinucleotide pool sizes during shoot initiation in tobacco callus. Plant Physiol., 65 : 587 - 590.

Brown, D. C. W. and Thorpe, T. A. 1980. Changes in water potential and its components during shoot formation in tobacco callus. Physiol. Plant. V.49: 83 - 97.

Burkill IH (1909) A working list of flowering plants of Baluchistan, by I.H. Burkill (Supriendent Govt. Printing, Calucatta)

Buyukalaca, S. and Mavituna, F., 1996. Somatic embryogenesis and plant regeneration of pepper in liquid media. Plant Cell Tiss. Org. Cult., 46 : 227 - 235.

Capellades, M. Lemeur, R. and Debergh, P. (1991). Effects of sucrose on starch accumulation and rate of photosynthesis in *Rosa* cultured *in vitro*. Plant Cell Tiss. Org. Cult. 25: 21-26.

Caplin, S.M. and Steward, F.C. (1948). Effect of coconutmilk on the growth of explants from carrot root. Science 108: 655-657.

Carman J.G. (1989). The *in ovulo* environment and its relevance to cloning wheat via somatic embryogenesis. *In vitro* Cell Dev. Biol, Plant. 25: 1155-1162.

Carneiro, L. A., Araujo, R. F. G., Brito, G. J. M., Fonseca, M. H. P. B., Costa, A., Crocomo, O. J. and Mansur, E. 1999. *In vitro* regeneration from leaf explants of *Neoreglia cruenta* (R. Graham) L.B.Smith, an endemic bromeliad from Easten Brazil. Plant Cell. Tiss. Org. Cult., 55 : 79 - 83.

Castellani C, Marai A, Vacchi P (1981) Bull Chem Farm 120: 570

Castiglioni, A. 1958. A History of Medicine". 2 nd ed. Alfred A. Knopf, New York.

Castillo, J.A. and Jordan, M. 1997. *In vitro* regeneration of *Minthostachys andian* (Brett), epling - a bolivian native species with aromatic and medicinal properties. Plant Cell Tiss. Organ Cult., 49 : 157 - 160.

Chakraborthy, T., Sinhababu, S.P. and Sukul, N.C. 1996. Preliminary evidence of antifilarial effect of *Centella asiatica* on canine dirofilariasis. Fitoterapia, 67 (2) : 110 - 112.

Chalupa, V. 1984. *In vitro* propagation of oak (*Quercus robur* L.) and linden (*Tilia cordata* Mill.). Biol. Plant., 26 : 374 - 377.

Chand, S., Sahrawat, A. K. and Prakash, D.V.S.S.R. 1997. *In vitro* culture of *Pimpinella anisum* L (anise). J. Plant Biochem. Biotech., 6 : 1 - 5.

Chao KH. Chung TJ, Kim SJ, Lee+ TH, Yoon CM (1981) Clinical experience of Madecassol (*Centella asiatica*) in the treatment of peptic ulcer. Korean Jour Gastroenterol 13(1): 49-56

Chao, K. H., Chang, T. J., Kim, S. J., Lee, T. H. and Yoon, C. M. 1981. Clinical experience of madecassal (*Centella asiatica*) in the treatment of peptic ulcer. Korean J. Gastroenterol. 13(1) : 49 - 56.

Chatterjee, T. K., Chakraborty, A. and Pathak, M. 1992. Effects of plant extract *Centella asiatica* (Linn.) on cold restraint stress ulcer in rats. Indian J. Experimental Biol., 30(10) : 889 - 891.

Chaturvedi, C., Mishra, P. and Jain, M. 1984. Proliferation of shoot tips and clonal multiplication of *Costus speciosus* in long term culture. Plant Sci. Lett., 35 : 67 - 71.

Chee, P. P. 1996. Plant regeneration from somatic embryos of *Taxus brevifolia*. Plant Cell Rep., 16 : 184 - 187.

Cheng M, His DCH and Phillips GC (1992) In vitro regeneration of Valencia-type peanut (Arachis hypogea L.) from cultured petioles, epicotyl sections and other seedling explants. Peanut Sci 19 : 82-87

Cho, H. J., Yang, W. Y., Lee, J. R., Park, Y. G. and Lee, S. Y. 1994. Plant regeneration through somatic embryogenesis of *Chidium officinale* Makino. RDA J. Agricultural Science Biotechnology, 36(1) : 165 - 172.

Chopra et al., (1949) Poisonous plants of India, by R.N.Chopra,R.L.Badhwar and S. Gosh (Govt Press Caluttta)

Chopra RN (1958) Chopra's indigenous Drug's of India, revised and largely rewritten by R.N. Chopra, I.C Chopra, K.L.Handa and L.D. Kapur (U.N.Dhur & sons private limited., Calcutta) 2nd edition.

Chopra SN, Badhuar RI, Ghosh S (ed) (1984) In: Poisonous plants of India. Vol.1, pp 513-514, Acodemic Publishers, Jaipur, India

Chopra, S. N., Badhwar, R. I. and Ghosh, S. (Eds) 1984. In: Poisonous plants of India Vol. 1 Pp 513 - 514, Academic Publishers, Jaipur, India.

Corrie, S. and Tandon, P. 1993. Propagation of *Cymbodium giganteum* wall. Through high frequency conversion of encapsulated protocorms under *in vivo* and *in vitro* conditions. Indian J. Exp. Biol. 31: 61- 64.

Cox, P. A., Rebecca, L., Sperry, Mervi, T. and Lass, B. 1989. Pharmacological activity of samoon ethnopharmacopocia. Econ. Bot., 43 : 487 - 497.

Damianl D, Faedi W and Cobianchi D (1983) . Nursery runner plant production, fruiting and behaviour of micropropagated strawberry plants. Acta Hort 131 : 193-197

Dandekar, U. P., Chandra, R. S., Dalvi, S. S., Joshi, M. V., Gokhale, P. C., Sharma, A. V., Shah, P. U. and Kshirsagar, N. A. 1992. Analysis of a clinically important interaction between phenytoin and Shankhapushpi, an ayurvedic preparation. Journal of Ethanopharmacology, 35(3): 285 - 288.

Danese, P., Carnevali, C. and Bertazzoni, M. G. 1994. Allergic contact dermatitis due to *Centella asiatica* extract. Contract Dermatitis, 31(3) : 201.

Darvathi, A. (1997). Aquatic plants - Their potential in Human Health. In: Solai Bulletin on Ethnopharmacology. Solai Programme at Vellore (Tamil Nadu) August, India.

Das Gupta, S. and Mandal, R. K. 1993. Compositional changes and storage protein synthesis in developing seeds of *Brassica campestris*. Seed Sci. Technol., 21 : 291 - 299.

Das, A. K. and Bhattacharjee, A. K. 1970. A systematic approach to phytochemical screening. Trop. Sci., 12 : 54 - 58.

Das, D. K., Shivaprakash, N. and Bhalla-Sarin, N. 1999. Multiple shoot induction and plant regeneration in litchi (*Litchi chinensis* Sonn.) Plant Cell Rep . 18 : 691-695

Das, P., Samantray, S., Roberts, A. V. and Rout, G. R. 1997. *In vitro* somatic embryogenesis of *Dalbergia sissoo* Roxb. A multipurpose timber yielding tree. Plant Cell Rep., 4 : 578 - 582.

Das, P., Timir, B. J. and Sumita, J. 1996. *In vitro* propagation of cashnewnut. Plant Cell Rep 15 : 615 - 619.

Das, T. and Mitra, G. C. 1990. Micropropagation of *Eucalyptus tereticornis* (Smith). Plant Cell Tiss. Org. Cult., 22 : 95 -103.

Datta K and Datta S.K. (1984). Rapid clonal multiplication on *Angelonia salicariefolia* through tissue culture. Plant Cell Tissue and Organ Culture 3: 215-220.

David, I. D., Debbie, P. L., Susan, I. K. and Trevor, A. T. 1992. Factors affecting recurrent shoot multiplication in *in vitro* cultures of 17 to 20 year old Douglas Fir Trees. *In vitro* Cell Dev. Biol., 28 : 33 -38.

Davies ME (1972) Polyphenol synthesis in cell suspension cultures of Paul's scarlet rose. Planta 104 : 50-65

Davies, M.E. (1972). Polyphenol synthesis in cell suspension cultures of Paul's scarlet rose. Planta., 104: 50-65.

De, A. J. J., Cordiwener, J., Loschiabo, F., Terzi, M., Vander Kerckhove, J., Van, K. A. and De, S. V. 1992. A carrot somatic embryo mutant is rescued by chitinase. Plant Cell., 4 : 425 - 433.

Demeke, T. and Hughes, H.G. (1990). Micropropagation of *Phytolacca dodecandra* through shoot tip and nodal cultures. Plant Cell Rep. 9: 390-392.

Dhar, U. and Upreti, J. 1999. *In vitro* regeneration of a mature leguminosus liana (*Bauhinia vahlii* W & A.). Plant Cell Rep., 18 : 664 - 669.

Dobos E, Danos B and Laszlo-Benesik A. (1994). Callus induction and shoot regeneration in *Sempervivum tectorum* Plant Cell Tissue and Organ Culture 36: 141-143.

Dodds JH and Roberts LW (1990) Induction of differentiation is xylem cells In : experiments in plant tissue culture. Cambridge. Univ Press. Pp 82-93

Dougall DK (1980) Nutrition and metabolism in plant tissue culture as a source of biochemicals. In : Plant tissue and culture as a source of biochemicals (Ed) E.J. Slaba CRC press, Boca Raton Florida, pp 115 - 122

Dougall, D.K. (1980). Nutrition and metabolism in plant tissue culture as a source of biochemicals, In: Plant Tissue and Culture as a source of Biochemicals (Ed.) E.J.Slaba, CRC Press, Boca Raton, Florida, pp. 115-122.

Drew, R. L. K. 1979. Effect of activated charcoal on embryogenesis and regenaration of plantlets from suspension cultures of carrot (*Daucus carota* L.). Ann. Bot. 44 : 387 - 389.

D'Silva, I. and D'Souza, L. 1992. *In vitro* propagation of *Anacardium occidentale* L. Plant Cell Tiss. Org. Cult., 29 : 1 - 6.

Du Manoir, J., Desmarest, P. and Saussay, R. 1985. *In vitro* propagation of fennel (*Foeniculum vulgare* Miller). Sci. Hortic., 27 : 5 - 19.

Duke, J. A. and Ayensu, E. S. 1985. Medicinal plants of China. Reference publication, Michigan, Pp 1 - 458.

Eapen S , George L and Rao PS (1993) Plant regeneration through somatic embryogenesis in peanut (Arachis hypogea L.) Biol Plant 35 : 499-504

Eapen S and George L (1990). Ontogeny of somatic embryos of Vigna aconitifolia, V. mungo and Vradiata. Ann Bot 66: 219-226

Eapen S and George L (1993) Plant regeneration from leaf discs of peanut and pigeonpea : Influence of benzyladenine, indole acetic acid and indole acetic acid - aminoacid conjugates. Plant Cell Tiss Org Cul 35: 223-227

Edwin, D., Geetha, V.R., Vishwanathan, H. and Usha Rani, M.V. 2000. Studies on the antimutagenic effects of *Centella asiatica*, A*lternanthera sessilis* and *Emblica officinalis* in somatic cells of max. J. of Environmental Biology 21(1): 75-78.

Ernst, D. 1983. Endogene cytokinin in einer zell suspensions kultur von Anis (*Pimpinella anisom* L.). Thesis, Ludwig-Maximilians-Univ. Munchen.

Ernst, D., Oesterhalt, D. and Schafer, W. 1984. Endogenesis cytokinins during embryogenesis in an anise cell culture (*Pimpinella anisum* L.). Planta, 161 : 240 - 245.

Ernst, D., Schafer, W. and Testerhelt, D. 1983b. Isolation and identification of a new, naturally occurring cytokinin (6-benzylamino purineriboside) from an anise cell culture *Pimpinella anisum* L.). Planta., 159 : 222 - 225.

Evans, D. A., Sharp, W. R. and Flick, C. E. 1981. Growth and behaviour of cell cultures: Embryogenesis and organogenesis. In: Plant tissue culture methods and applications in agriculture. Thorpe, T. A. (Ed.), Academic Press, London. Pp 45 - 114.

Fakim, A. G. and Swaraj, M. D. 1990. A systemic approach to phytochemical screening. Trop. Sci., 12 : 54 - 58.

Farnsworth, N.R. (1966). Biological and phytochemical screening of plants. J. Pharm. Sci. 55: 225-226.

Fowler MW (1983) Primary and secondary metabolisms of cell cultures In: Plant biotechnology, primary and secondary metabolisms of plant cell cultures (Eds.) S.H. Mantell and H. Smith, Cambridge University Press. London pp 37

Fowler, M.W. (1983). Primary and secondary metabolisms of cell cultures, In: Plant Biotechnology, primary and secondary metabolisms of plant cell cultures (Eds.) S.H. Mantell and H.Smith, Cambridge University Press, London, pp.37.

Furuya T (1978) . Biotransformation of cardiac glycosides through plant cell cultures In : Frontiers of plant tissue culture, International association for plant tissue culture, (Ed) T.A. Thorpe, University of Calgary, Calgary, pp 191

Furya, T. (1978). Biotransformation of cardiac glycosides through plant cell cultures, In: Frontiers of Plant Tissue Culture, International Association for Plant Tissue Culture, (Ed.) T.A.Thorpe, University of Calgary, Calgary, pp 191.

Gamborg, O., Miller, R. and Ojima, K. 1968. Nutrient requirement of suspension cultures of soybean root cells. Exp. Cell Res. 50: 151-158.

Gamborg, O.L., Murashig, T., Thorpe, T. A. and Vasil, J. K. 1976. Plant tissue culture media. *In vitro*, 12 : 473 - 478.

Garcia-Rodriguez, M. J., Paupardin, C. and Saussay, R. 1978. Sur la formation d'um tissue secreteur et la synthese d'anethole par des tissues de Fenocil (*Foeniculum vulgare* Mill. Var. duice) cultives *In vitro.* CR Acad. Sci. Paris, 287 : 693 - 696.

Gauheret RJ (1985) . History of plant tissue and cell culture. A personal account. In : I.K. Vasil (Eds.) , cell culture and somatic cell genetics of plants. Orlando, Academic Press pp 2-59

Gautheret, R.J. (1947). Sur quelques particularites des actions morphogeneses exercees par les acides 2,4-dichloro phenoxyacetique et naphtoxyacetique. Comptes Rendus la societe de Biologia 141: 560-563.

George PS, Ravishankar GA, Venkataraman LV (1993) Clonal multiplication of *Gardenia jasminoides* Ellis through axillary bud culture. Plant Cell Rep 13: 59-62

George, E. F. and Sherrington, P.D . 1984. Plant propagation by tissue culture. Exegetics, England.

George, F. E. 1993. In: Plant propagation by tissue culture. Exegetics Ltd., Edington, England. Pp 1 - 580.

George, F. E. and Sen, S. 1992. Stable regeneration in *Asparagus cooperi* baker as controlled by different factors. Plant Sci., 82 : 119 - 124.

Ghani, A. 1998. Medicinal plants of Bangladesh. Asiatic Society of Bangladesh, Dhaka, Bangladesh.

Ghimire, G. P. S. and Bhattarai, M. D. 1990. Net aerial production of ground flora in phulchowki Himalaya, Kathmandu (Nepal). Journal of Economic Botany and Phytochemistry, 1(1) : 35 - 38.

Ghosh, B, and Sen, S. 1994b. Plant regeneration from alginate encapsulated somatic embryos from *Asparagus cooperi* Baker. Plant Cell Rep., 13 : 381 - 385.

Ghosh, B. and Sen, S. (1994). Micropropagation of *Asparagus cooperei* Baker as affected by growth regulators. Bio Plant. 36: 527-534.

Ghosh, B. and Sen, S. 1994a. Micorpropagation of *Asparagus cooperi* Baker as affected by growth regulators. Bio. Plant., 36 : 527 - 534.

Girija S, Ganapathi A and Ananthakrishnan G (2000) Somatic embryogenesis in *Vigna radiata* (L.) Wilczek. Indian J. Exp. Biol. 38: 1241-1244.

Glasby, J. S. 1991. Dictionary of plants containing secondaly metabolities, Taylor and Francis, London. Pp 1 - 488.

Gleddie, S., Keller, W. and Setterfield, G. 1983. Somatic embryogenesis and plant regeneration from leaf explant and cell suspensions of *Solanum melongena.* Can. J. Bot., 61: 656 - 666.

Goel RK, Maiti RN, Manikam M and Ray AB (1997) Antiulcer activity of naturally occurring pyrano-coumarin and isocumarins and their effect on prostanoid synthesis using human colonic mucosa. Ind J Exp Biol 35 : 1080-1083

Goel, R.K. Maiti, R.N. Manickam, M and Ray, A.B. (1997). Antiulcer activity of naturally occurring pyrano-coumarin and isocoumarins and their effect on prostanoid synthesis using human colonic mucosa. Ind. J. exp. Biol. 35: 1080-1083.

Gomez, K.Z. and Gomex, K.Z. 1976. Statistical procedure for agricultural research with emphasis of rice. Los Bans. Phillipines Internation Rice Research Institute.

Gosal SS and Bajaj YPS (1979) Establishment of callus tissue culture and the introduction of organogenesis in some grain legumes . Crop Improv. 6 : 154-160

Govind J, Kapadia N, and Shah J (1992) Isolation of quaternary alkaloids of Magnolia acuminata Ind J Pharm Sci 54 : 142-144

Govind, J., Kapadia, N. and Shah, J. (1992). Isolatioin of quaternary alkaloids of *Magnolia acuminata* Ind. J. Pharm. Sci., 54: 142-144.

Gras, M. C. S. and Calvo, M. C. 1996. Micropropogation of *Lavandual latifolia* through nodal bud culture of mature plants. Plant Cell Tiss. Org. Cult., 45 : 259 - 261.

Gray, D. J. and Purohit, A. 1991. Somatic embryogenesis and development of synthetic seed technology. Crit. Rev. Plant Sci., 10 : 33 - 61.

Guha Bakshi DN, Sensarma P, Pal OC (1999) A Lexicon of Medicinal Plants in India. NayaProkash, Calcutta, India

Gulati A and Jaiwal PK (1990) Culture conditions effecting plant regeneration from cotyledons of Vigna radiata (L.) Wilzek. Plant Cell Tiss Org Cul 23: 1-7

Gulati, A, and Jaiwal, P. K. 1994. Plant regeneration from cotyledonary node explants of mung bean (*Vigna radiata).* Plant Cell Rep. 13: 523-527.

Gulati, A. and Jaiwal, P. K. 1992. *In vitro* induction of multiple shoots and plant regeneration from shoot tips of mung bean *(Vigna radiata).*Plant Cell. Tiss.Org. Cult. 29 : 199 - 205.

Gupta S.K. Srivastava A.K. Singh P.K. and Tuli, R. (1997). *In vitro* proliferation of shoots and regeneration of cotton. Plant Cell Tissue and Organ Culture 51: 149-152.

Gupta, A.P. Gupta, M.M. and Sushil Kumar (1999). High performance thin layer chromatography of asiaticoside in *Centella asiatica*. Journal of Indian Chemical Society. 76: 321 - 322.

Gupta, O. P., Srivastva, T. N., Gupta, S. C. and Badola, D.P. (1980a). An ethnobotanical and phytochemical screening of high altitude plants of Ladhak-I. Bull.Medico- Ethnobot.Res., 2 : 301 - 317.

Gupta, O.P. Srivastava, T.N. Gupta, S.C and Badola, D.P. (1980b). Ethnobotanical and phytochemical screening of high altitude plants of Ladhak-II. Bull. Medico-Ethnobot. Res. 2: 301-317.

Gupta, O.P. Srivastava, T.N. Gupta, S.C. and Badola, D.P. (1980a). An ethonobotanical and phytochemical screening of high altitude plants of Ladhak-II. Bull. Medico-Ethnobot. Res.1: 301-317.

Gupta, O.P., Srivastva, T.N.,Gupta, S.C. and Badola, D.P. (1980b).Ethnobotanical and phytochemical screening of high altitude plants of Ladhak- II. Bull.Medico- Ethnobot.Res.2:67-88.

Gupta, P. K., Nadgir, A. L, Mascarenhas, A. F. and Jagannathan V (1980). Tissue culture of forest trees: clonal multiplication of Tectona grandis L. (Teak) by tissue culture. Plant Sci. Lett., 17: 259 - 268.

Gupta, S. K., A. K. Srivastava, P. K. Singh and Rakesh, T. 1997. *In vitro* proliferation of shoots and regeneration of cotton. Plant Cell. Tiss. Org.Cult. 51 : 149 - 152.

Gurib-Fabin, A., Gueho, J. and Seuraj Biossondoyal, M. 1997. Int. J. Pharmacognosy, 35: 244.

Haberlandt G (1902) Cultureversuche mit isolierten pflanzenzellen . Situngsber . Math. Naturwiss . Kl. Kais. Akad. Wien . 111 : 69-92

Hahlbrock K (1977) In : Plant tissue culture and its biotechnological applications (Eds.) W.Barz, E. Reinhard and M.H. Zenk, Springer -Verlag, Berlin and New york, pp 95-111

Hahlbrock, K. (1977). In: Plant Tissue Culture and its Biotechnological Appliction (Eds.) W.Barz, E.Reinhard and M.H.Zenk, Springer-Verlag, Berlin and New York, pp.95-111.

Halperin, W. and Wetherell, D. R. 1964. Adventive embryony in tissue cultures of the wild carrot *Dacas carota*. Am. J. Bot., 51 : 274 - 288.

Handa, S. S. 1994. Rasayana drugs part-II Pharma Times, 26(3) : 17 - 25.

Handique, P. J. and Bora, P. 1999. *In vitro* regeneration of a medicinal plant - *Houttuynia cordata* Thunb. from nodal explants. Curr. Sci. 6 : 1245 - 1247.

Harborne, J. B. 1984. (Eds.) Phytochemical methods, Chapman and Hall, London.

Hay CA, Anderson LA, Roberts, MF and Phillipson JD (1988) Plant tissue culture as a source of biomedicals, In : Advances in biotechnological processes (Eds .) A. Mizrahi and A.L. Van Wezel, Alan, R. Liss Inc, New york

Hay, C.A., Anderson, L.A., Roberts, M.F. and Phillipson, J.D. (1988). Plant Tissue culture as a source of Biomedicals, In : Advances in Biotechnological processes (Eds.) A.Mizrahi and A.L.Van Wezel, Alan, R.Liss Inc., New York.

Hicks GS (1980) Patterns of organ development in plant tissue culture and the problem of organ determination . Bot. Rev. 46 : 1-23

Hiraoka, N. 1989. *Bupleurum falcatum* L. Embryogenesis and the production of Saikosaponins. In: Bajaj YPS (ed) Biotechnology in Agriculture and Forestry. V 7 (pp 69-81). Springer-Verlag, Berlin, Heidelberg.

Hiraoka, N., Kasahara, M., Sasahi, K. and Iton, A. 1995. Natural medicines 49(2) : 197 - 199. Cold storage of Glehria littoralis shoots cultured *in vitro*.

Hong W and Debergh P (1995). Somatic embryogenesis and plant regeneration in garden leek. Plant Cell Tissue and Organ Culture 43: 21-28.

Hossain M, Biswas BK, Karim MR, Rahman S, Islam R, Joarder O (1994) *In vitro* organogenesis of elephant apple (*Feronia limonia*). Plant Cell Tissue Org Cult 39: 265-268

Hossain, M., Rahman, S. M. Islam, R. and Joarder, O. I. 1993. High frequency plant regeneration from petiole explants of *Carica papaya* L. through organogenesis. Plant Cell Rep., 13 : 99 - 102.

Hossain, S. N., Rahman, S., Joydhar, A., Islam, S. and Hossain, M. 2000. *In vitro* propagation of Thankuni (*Centella asiatica* L.). Plant. Tiss. Cult.,. 10(1) : 17 - 23.

Hossain, S.N., Rahman, S., Toydhar, A., Islam, S. and Hossain, H. 2000. *In vitro* propagation of Thankuni *Centella asiatica* (L.). Plant Tissue Culture, 10(1) : 17 - 23.

Huber, J., Constabel, F. and Gamborg, O. L . 1978. A cell-counting procedure applied to embroyogenesis in cell suspension cultures of anise (*Pimpinella anisum* L.) Plant Sci. Lett 12: 209-215.

Hunault, G. 1981. La culture *In vitro* des tissue de Fenouil (*Foeniculum vulgare* Mill.). Premieres observations Sur le comportement des explants primitifs et des cals. CR Acad. Sci. Paris, 293 : 553 - 555.

Hunault, G. 1984. *In vitro* culture of fennel tissues *Foeniculum vulgare* Mill. from cell suspension to mature plant. Sci. Hortic., 22 : 55 - 65.

Hunault, G. and Du Manoir, J. 1992. Micropropagation of Fennel (*Foeniculum vulgare* Mill.). In: Bajaj, Y. P. S. (ed) Biotechnology in Agriculture and Forestry. V. 19. Pp 199 - 218. Springer-Verlag Berlin, Heidelberg.

Hunault, G. Desmaresr, P. and Du Manoir J. 1989. *Foeniculum vulgare* Mill. Cell culture, regeneration and the production of anethole. In: Bajaj YPS (ed) Biotechnology in Agriculture and Forestry, Vol. 7 (pp 185-212). Springer-Verlag, Berlin, Heidelber.

Hussey, G. 1986. Problems and prospects in the *in vitro* propagation of herbaceous plants. In: Plant tissue culture and its agricultural application. Withers, L. A. and Anderson, P. G. (eds.), Butterworths, London. Pp 69 - 84.

Ignacimuthu, S., Arokiasamy, S., Antonysamy, M. and Ravichandran, P. 1999. Plant regeneration through somatic embryogenesis from mature leaf explants of *Eryngium foetidum,* a contiment. Plant Cell Tiss. and Org. Cult., 56 : 131 - 137.

In : Frontiers of plant tissue culture (Ed.) T.A. Thorpe, The Book store, University of Calgary, Alberta Canada pp 297-306

Janosi, H., Mathe, A. and Mozrar, K. 1991. Contribution to the micropropogation of triploid water melon. Acta. Hort. 300: 63-108.

Jha S and Jha TB (1989). Micropropagation of *Cephaelis ipecacuanha.* Plant Cell Rep. 8: 437-439.

Jha S and Sen S (1985). Regeneration and rapid multiplication of Bowiea volubilis Harv. in tissue culture. Plant Cell Rep. 4: 1, 12-14.

Johannson L and Eriksson T. (1984). Effects of carbon dioxide in anther cultures. Physiol Plant, 60 : 26-30

Jordan, M. and Balbao, O. (1985). *In vitro* regeneration of *Prosopis tamarugo* Phil. and *Prosopis chilensis* (Mol.) Stuntz from nodal sections. Gartenbauwissenschaft, 50: 138-142.

Jordan, M., Pedraza, J. and Goreux, A. 1985. *In vitro* propagation studies of three *Prosopis* species (*P. chilensis, P. alba* and *P. tamarugo*) through shoot tip culture. Gartenbauwissenschaft, 50 : 265 - 267.

Joshi, V., Merhant, J. R., Nadakany, V. V., Namboori, K. and Vaghani, D. D. 1974. Chemical components of some Indian medicinal plants. Ind. J. Chem., 12 : 226.

Kamar, M. G. and Rao, P. S. 1978. Vegetative multiplication of egg plants (*Solanum melangena*) using tissue culture techniques. Plant Sci. Lett., 13 : 57 - 65.

Kao KN and Michyluk MR (1981) Embryoid formation in alfalfa cell suspension cultures from different plant. In vitro 17: 645-648

Karnick, C.R. 1989. Studies on standardization of ayurvedic crude drugs. Series X-brahmy-*Hydrocotyle asiatica* Linn. Syn: *Centella asiatica* (Linn.) Urban. Indian Medicine, 1(2) : 21 - 23.

Karting T (1988) Craker LE and Simon JE (eds) Clinical Application of *Centella asiatica* (L.) Urb. In Herbs, Spices and medicinal Plants

Kataeva, N. V. and Popowich, E. A. 1993. Maturation and rejuvenation of Coriandrum sativum shoot clones during micropropagation. Plant Cell Tiss. and Org. Cult., 34 : 141 - 148.

Khlifi S and Tremblay FM (1995). Maturation of black spruce somatic embryos. Part I. Effect of L-glutamine on the number and germinability of somatic embryos. Plant Cell Tiss. Org. Cult. 41: 23-32.

Kim, K. S., Pack, T. W., Ko, K. M., Hwang, S. S., Jm, H. T. and Hwang, H. 1995. Multiplication and transformation of medicinal plants for production of useful secondary metabolities a) plant regeneration from petiole explants of *Centella asiatica* (L.) urban *In vitro* cultures. Journal of Plant Biology, 38(2) : 211 - 215.

Kirtikar, K R, B.D.Basu & I.C.S. (retd.);Indian medicinal plants, revised by E.Blatter, J.F.Caius & K.S.Mhaskar (Lalit Mohan Basu, Allahabad), 4 Vols., 2nd edn,1935.

Kokate CK (1995) Medicinal and aromatic plants Advancesc in horticultureYl : (eds) K.L.Chandra and R.Gupta, Malhotra publishing house New Delhi, pp 223-248

Kokate, C.K. (1995). Medicinal and Aromatic Plants. Advances in Horticulture Vol. 11 (Eds.) K.L. Chandha and R.Gupta, Malhotra Publishing Huse, New Delhi, pp.223-248.

Komalavalli, N. and Rao, M. V. 2000. *In vitro* micropropagation of *Gymnema sylvestre* - A multipurpose medicinal plant. Plant Cell. Tiss. Org. Cult., 61 : 97 - 105.

Komalavalli, N. and Rao, M.V. (1997). *In vitro* micropropagation of *Gymnema elegans* W & A, a rare medicinal plant. Indian J. Exp. Biol. 35: 1088-1092.

Komamine, A., Kawara, R., Matsumoto, M., Sunabori, S., Toya, G. and Fujimura, T. 1992. Mechanism of somatic embryogenesis in cell cultures. *In vitro* Cell Dev. Bio., 35 : 1088 - 1092.

Krens, F.A., Keizer, L. C. P. and Capel, I. E. M. 1997. Transgenic caraway, *Carum carvi* L. a model species for metabolic engineering.Plant Cell. Rep., 17: 39-43.

Krens, F.A., Trifonova, A., Keizer, L.C.P. and Hall, R.D. 1996. The effect of exogenously-applied phytohormones on gene transfer efficiency in sugarbeet (*Beta vulgaris* L.) Plant Sci. 116: 97-106.

Krishnan Lal, Kalsi, R., Sharma, A. and Handa, S. S. 1994. HPLC analysis of asiaticoside in *Centella asiatica*. Indian Journal of pharmaceutical Sciences, 56(4) : 154.

Krishnan, P. N., Sudha, C. G. and Seeni, S. 1995. Rapid micropropagation through shoot tip culture of *Trichopus zeylanicus* Gaertn., a rare ethnomedicinal plant. Plant Cell Rep., 14 : 708 - 711.

Krishnan, P.N. and Seeni, S. (1994). Rapid micropropagation of *Woodfordia fruticosa* (L.) Kurz (Lythraceae), a rare medicinal plant. Plant Cell Rep. 14: 55-58.

Kritikar KR and Basu BD (1935) Indian medicinal plants, by K.R.Kritikar , B.D. Basu & an I.C.S (retd,) : revised by E. Blatter, J.F. Caius and K.S. Mhaskar (Lalit Mohan Basu, Allahabad) 4 vols ., 2nd edn .

Krul WR, (1993) Enhancement and repression of somatic embryogenesis in cell cultures of carrot by cold pretreatment of stock plants . Plant Cell Tiss . Org. Cul. 32 : 271-276

Kudielka, R. A. and Theimer, R. R. 1983a. Somatic embroyogenesis in anise (*Pimpinella anisum* L.) cell cultures in microcavity environment. Proc worksh Space Biology, Coloyne, Germany, ESASP - 206, Pp 63 - 68.

Kukreja AK, Mathur AK (1985) Tissue culture studies in *Duboisia myoporoides* I. Plant regeneration and clonal propagation by stem node cultures. Planta Med 2: 93-96

Kulothangan, S. 1997. *In vitro* culture studies on cowpea (*Vigna unguiculata* (L.) Walp.). Ph.D. Thesis, Bharathidasan University, Tiruchirappalli, India.

Kulothungan S, Ganapathi A, Shajahan A and Kathiravan K (1995) Somatic embryogenesis in cell suspension culture of cow pea (Vigna unguiculata (L.) Walp) Israel J. Plant Sci 43: 385-390

Kumar AS, Gamborg OL and Nabors MW (1988) Regeneration from long-term cell suspension cultures of tepry bean (Phaseolus acutifolius) Plant Cell Rep 7: 322-325

Kumar, V., Bose, S. and Gupta V. K. 2000. *Centella asiatica,* a memory-enhancing agent has no cholinergic action on isolated guinea pig ileum. Indian J. Pharmacology, 32(1) : 73 - 74.

Kuppurajan, K. 1995. Anti-anxiety effect of an ayurvedic compound preparation-A cross over trial. Seminar on Research In Ayurveda and Siddha CCRAS, New Delhi, 40 : 20 - 22.

Kuppurajan, K., Seshadri, C., Rajagopalan, V., Srinivasan, K., Sitaraman, R., Indurthi, J. and Venkataraghavan, S. 1992. Anti-anxiety effect of an ayurvedic compound drug-a cross over trial. Journal of Research in Ayurveda and Siddha, 13(3-4) : 107 - 116.

Lakshmanan, P., Lee, C. L. and Goh, C. J. 1997. An efficient *in vitro* method for mass propagation of a woody ornamental *Ixora coccinea* L. Plant Cell Rep., 16 : 572 - 577.

Lal N, Ahuja PS (1989) Propagation of Indian Rhubarb (*Rheum emodi* Watt) using shoot tip and leaf explant culture. Plant Cell Rep 8: 493-496

Lazzeri PA, Hidlebrand Df, and Collins GB (1985). A procedure for plant regeneration from immature cotyledon tissue of soyabean Pl Mole Bio Rep 3: 160-167

Lazzeri PA, Hidlebrand Df, and Collins GB (1987) Soyabean somatic embryogenesis : effect of hormones and culture manipulation. Plant Cell Tiss Org Cul 10: 197-208

Litz, R. E. and Gray, D. J. 1992. Organogenesis and somatic embryogenesis. In: Biotechnology of perennial fruit crops. Hammerschalg, F. A. and Litz, R. E. (Reds.), CAB International, The Netherlands. Pp 3 - 34.

Litz, R. E. and Gray, D. J. 1995. Somatic embryogenesis for agricultural improvement. World J. Microbiol. Biotech., 11 : 416 - 425.

Lucia, R., De-Sertie, J. A. A., Camargo, E. A. and Pannizza, S. 1997. Pharmacological and toxicological studies on *Centella asiatica* extract. Fitoterpia, 68(5) : 413 - 416.

Lundergan, C. A. and Janick, J. 1980. Regulation of apple shoot proliferation and growth *in vitro*. Hortic. Res., 20 : 19 - 24.

Luz, J. M. Q., Pasqual, M., De-Souza, R. J. and Nogueira, A. M. .M. 1994. *In vitro* propagation of peruvien carrot (*Arracacia xanthorrhiza* Bancroft). Ciencia e Pratica, 18(4) : 339 - 402.

Malathy Suryanarayanan, Jagadish S Pai (1998) Studies in micropropagation of *Coleus forskohlii*. J of Medicinal and Arom Pl Sciences 20: 379-382

Mandi, K.K. and Sharma, A.K. (1994). Chemical constituents of Zingiberaceae taxonomic makers: A review. Nucleus, 37: 123-131.

Manjula S, Anju J and Nair G.M. (2000) Somatic embryogenesis from leaf derived callus of *Tylophora indica* (Burm.f.) Merill. Indian J. Exp. Biol. 38: 1069-1072.

Manjula, S., Anita, T. Benny, D. and Nair, G. M. 1997. *In vitro* plant regeneration of *Aristolochia indica* through axillary shoot multiplication and organogenesis. Plant Cell, Tiss. Org. Cult., 51 : 145 - 148.

Marascuilo LA, McSweeney M (1977) Non-Parametric and Distribution free methods for the social sciences. Books/cole Publ CA pp 141-147

Martindale (1955). The extra pharmacipoeia. The pharmaceutical press, London, Vol.I, 24th edn,

Masuda, H., Oohashi, S. I., Tokuji, Y. and Mizue, Y. 1995. Direct embryo formation from epidermal cells of carrot hypocotyls. Journal of plant physiology, 145(4) : 531 - 534.

Mathew, P. J. and Unithan, M. C. 1992. Search for plants having anticancer properties used by the tribals of wynadu, malapuram and palghat districts of Keral, India. Aryavaidyan, 6(1) : 54 - 60.

Mathur A, Mathur AK, Kukreja AK, Ahuja PS, Tyagi BR (1987) Establishment and multiplication of colchi autotetraploids of *Rauvolfia serpentina* L. Plant Cell Tiss Org Cult 10: 129-134

Mc Kently, A. H., Moore, G. A. and Gardner, F. P. 1990. *In vitro* plant regeneration of peanut from seed explants. Crop Sci., 30 : 192 - 196.

McNichol RJ and Graham J (1990) In vitro regeneration of Rubus from leaf and stem segments Plant Cell Tiss Org. Cul 21 : 45-50

McWilliam, A. A., Smith, S. M. and Street, H. E. 1974. The origin and development of embryoids in suspension cultures of carrot (*Daucus carota*). Ann. Bot., 38 : 243 - 250.

Mendoza, A. B. and Futsuhara, Y. 1990. Varietal differences on plant regeneration by tissue culture in mung bean (*Vigna radiata).* Jap. J. Breed., 40 : 457 - 467.

Mendoza, A. B., Hattori, K. and Futsuhara, Y. 1992. Shoot regeneration from the callus immature primary leaves in mung bean (*Vigna radiata*). Jap. J. Breed., 42 : 145 - 149.

Mercier H, Vieira CCJ, Figueredo-Ribeiro RCL (1992) Tissue culture and plant propagation of *Gomphrena officinalis* a Brazillian medicinal plant. Plant Cell Tiss Org Cult 28: 249-254

Micher SA and Bauer EO (1991) High frequency of somatic embryogenesis from leaf tissue from Populus spp . Plant Sci 77: 111-118

Miller, C.O. (1961). Kinetin related compounds in in morden methods of plant analysis b : (ED) Linskens and tracy, Springer-Verlag Berlin pp 194 - 202.

Minocha, S. C. 1987. Plant growth regulators and morphogenesis in cell and tissue culture of forest trees. In: Bonga, J. M. and Durzan, D. J. (eds) Cell and Tissue culture in forestry. Vol 1. Martinus Nijhoff, The Hague, pp 56 - 59.

Miura, Y. and Tabuta, M. 1986. Direct somatic embryogenesis from protoplasts of *Foeniculum vulgare*. Plant Cell Rep., 5 : 310 - 313.

Mohamed, S. V., Jawahar, M., Thiruvengadam, M., Jeyakumar, M. and Jayabalan, N. 1999. Effect of cytokinins on the proliferation of multiple shoots in Horse gram (*Macrotyloma uniflorum* (Linn). Verdc.). J. Plant Biotech., 1: 79 - 83.

Mondal, M. Gupta, S. and Mukherjee, B.B. (1990). *In vitro* propagation of shoot buds of *Carcia papaya* L. (Caricaceae) Var. Honey Dew. Plant Cell Rep. 8: 609-612.

Moosa, J. S., Al-Yahya, M. A., Al-Meshal, I. A. and Tariq, M. 1983. Pytochemical and biological screening of Saudi medicinal plant-parts. Fitoter., 54 : 147 - 152.

Morel GM (1960) Producing virus free cymbidium Amer. Orchid Soc. Bull .29: 495-497

Morel GM (1975) Clonal multiplication of orchids. In : (C.L. Wintert (Eds.) The orchids-scientific studies pp 169-222

Mroginski, L.A. and Kartha, K.K. (1984). Tissue culture of Legumes for crop improvement. Plant Breed. Rev. 2: 215-264.

Mroginski, L.A., Kartha, K.K. and Shyluk, J.P. 1981. Regeneration of peanut plantlets by *in vitro* culture of immature leaves. Can. J. Bot. 59: 826-830.

Muralidharan, E. M and Mascarenhas, A. F. 1987. *In vitro* plantlet formation by organogenesis in *Eucalyptus camaldulensis* and by somatic embryogenesis in *E. citriodora*. Plant Cell Rep., 6 : 256 - 259.

Murashige T, Skoog F (1962) A revised medium for rapid growth and bioassay with tobacco tissue culture. Physiologia Pl 15: 473-497

Murashige, T. 1974. Plant propagation through tissue cultures. Ann. Rev. Plant Physiol., 25 : 136 - 166.

Murat, O., Sebahattin, O., Cafer, S. S., Cengiz, S. and Mustafa, Y. 1998. High frequency adventitious shoot regeneration in sainfoin. Plant Cell Tiss. Org.Cult., 52 : 205 - 208.

Nalini, K., Arror, A. R., Karanth, K. S. and Rao, A. 1992. Effect of *Centella asiatica* fresh leaf aqueous extract on learning memory and biogenic amine turnover in albino rats. Fitoterapia, 63(3) : 232 - 237.

Nandi, R. P., Amang, B. K. and Chatterjee, S. K. 1985. Phytochemical studies on some ethnomedicinal plants growing in the foot hills of Eastern Himalayas. Proc. (Spl. Issue). Vth ISHS, Symp. Med. Arom. Spice. Pp. 131 - 135.

Narashimulu SB and Reddy GM (1983) Plantlet regeneration from different callus cultures of *Arachis hypogea* L. Plant Sci Lett 31 : 147-153

Narayanaswamy, S. (1994). Plant Cell and tissue culture. tata McGraw Hill Publ. Co. Ltd., New Delhi, pp 1-514.

Nautiyal, S. and Semwal, J. K. 1984. Screening of some Himalayan Alpine plants for alkaloids, flavonoids and saponins. Indian drugs, 21 : 425 - 430.

Nichol JW, Slade D , Viss P and Stuart DA (1991) Effect of organic acid pre-treatment on the regeneration and development (conversion) of whole plants from callus cultures of alfala, Medicago sativa L. Plant Sci 79 : 181-192

Nitsch C, Nitsch JP (1967) The induction of flowering *in vitro* in stem segments of *Plambago indica* L. 1 The production of vegetative buds. Planta 72: 355-370

Normah, M.N., Hamidah, S. and Ghani, F. D. 1997. Micropropagation of *Citrus halimii* - an endangered species of South-East Asia. Plant Cell Tiss. Org. Cult., 50 : 225 - 227.

Norstog K and Klein RM (1972). Development of cultured barely embryos. II Precocious germination and dormancy. Can. J. Bot. 50: 1887-1894.

Odebiyi, P. P. and Sofowora, E. A. 1978. Phytochemical screening of Nigerian medicinal plants II. Lloydia, 41: 234 - 240.

Ono, Y., Takahata Y. and Kaizuma, N. (1994). Effect of genotype on shoot regeneration from cotyledonary explants of rapeseed (*Brassica napus* L.) Plant Cell Rep. 14: 13-17.

Ozgen M, Ozcan S, Sevimay S.C., Sancak C and Yildiz M. (1998). High frequency adventitious shoot regeneration in sainfoin. Plant Cell Tissue and Organ Culture 52: 205-208.

Ozias-Akins, P., Anderson, W. F. and Holbrock, C. C. 1992. Somatic embryogenesis in *Arachis hypogaea* L. genotype comparison. Plant Sci., 83 : 103 - 111.

Pareek, L. K. and Swarnkar, P. L. 1997. Trends in plant tissue culture and biotechnology. Agrobotanical Publ. India. Pp 1 - 334.

Parnham MJ (1996) Plant as a source of active drugs. Drug News Perspect 9: 508-511

Parnham, M. J. 1996. Plant as a source of active drugs. Drugs News Perscpet, 9 : 508 - 511.

Patel, M.B. Bhardwaj, R. and Joshi, A. 1991. Organogenesis in *Vigna radiata* (L.) Wilczek, Indian J. Exp. Biol. 29: 619-621.

Patil, J. S., Nagavi, B. G., Ramesh, M. and Vijayakumar, G. S. 1998. A study on the immunostimulant activity of *Centella asiatica* Linn. in rats. Indian drugs, 35(11) : 711 - 714.

Patra, A., Rai, B., Rout, G. R. and Das, P. 1998. Successful plant regeneration from callus cultures of *Centella asiatica* (Linn.) Urban. Plant Growth Regulation, 24 : 13 - 16.

Pattnaik SK, Chand PK (1996) *In vitro* propagation of the medicinal herbs *Ocimum americanum* L. syn. *O. camom.* Sims (hoary basil) and *Ocimum sanctum* L. (holy basil). Plant Cell Rep 15: 846-850

Pattnaik, J. and Debata, B.K. (1996). Micropropagation of *Hemidesmus indicus* (L.) Br. through axillary bud culture. Plant Cell Rep. 15: 427-430.

Pattnaik, S. and Chand, K. .P 1996. *In vitro* propagation of the medicinal herbs (*Ocimum americanum* L. Syn. *Ocimum canum* Sims. (hoary basil) and *O. sanctum* L. (holy basil). Plant Cell Rep., 15 : 846 - 850.

Pattnaik, S. K. and Chand, P. K. 1997. Rapid clonal propagation of three mulberries, *Morus cathayana* Hemsl., *M. Ihou Koiz* and *M. serrata* Roxb., through *in vitro* culture of apical shoot buds and nodal explants from mature trees. Plant Cell Rep., 16 : 503 - 508.

Paupardin, C. 1976. Sur la differentiation d'un tissu secreteur et la formation d'huile essentielle par des tissues vegetaux cultives *In vitro.* Actes lol e congr Soc Savantes, Lille, France, Pp 629 - 641.

Paupardin, C., Garcia-Rodriguez, M. J. and Bricout, J. 1980. Multiplication vegetative de quelaues plantes arometiques: Problemes poces par la production d'essence CR Acad. Agric. For., 66 : 658 - 666.

Perera, K. D. A. 1990. Characterization and evaluation of bush type of *Centella asiatica*. Tropical Agriculturist, 146 : 127 - 131.

Plohmann, B., Bader, G., Streich, S., Hiller, K. and Franz, G. 1994. Immunomodulatory effects of triterpenoid saponins. European Journal of Pharmaceutical Sciences, 2(1-2) : 120.

Prakash E, Sha Valli Khan P.S. Sairam Reddy P and Rao K.R. (1999). Regeneration of plants from seed-derived callus of *Hybanthus enneaspermus* L. Muell., a rare ethonobotanical herb. Plant Cell Rep. 18: 873-878.

Prem, L. B. and Xu, H. 1999. Plant regeneration from callus of Australian fan flower, Scaevola. J. Plant Physiol., 154 : 374 - 378.

Purdit, .M., Paud, D., Dalta, A. and Srivastava, P. S. 1995. *In vitro* flowering and high xanthotoxin in Ammi majus L. J. Plant Biochemistry and Biotechnology, 4(2) : 73 - 76.

Purohit S.D. Dave A and Kukda G. (1994). Micropropagation of safed musli (*Chlorophytum borivilianum*) a rare Indian medicinal herb. Plant Cell Tissue and Organ Culture 39: 93-96.

Purohit, .M., Paude, D., Dalta, A. and Srivastava, P. S. 1995. Enhanced Xanthotoxin content in regenerating cultures of *Ammi majus* and micropropagation. Planta Medica, 61(5) : 481 - 482.

Quraishi, A. and Mishra, S.K. (1998). Micropropagation of nodal explants from adult trees of *Cleistanthus collinus*. Plant Cell Rep. 17: 430-433.

Rajagopalan, V. 1995. Effect of Ayushman-8 in Manasa mandata (mental retardation). Seminar on Research in Ayurveda and Siddha. CCRAS, New Delhi. p34, 20-22.

Ramaswamy, A. S., Periasamy, S. M. and Basu, N. 1970. Pharmacological studies on *Centella asiatica* L. (Bramamanduki). Jour. Res. Ind. Med., 4(2) : 160 - 173.

Ramdev Reddy, I and Reddy, G.M. (1993). Factors affecting direct somatic embryogenesis and plant regeneration in groundnut (*Arachis hypogaea* L.) Indian J. Exp. Biol. 31: 57-60.

Ramesh Anbazhagan V and Ganapathi A (1999) Somatic embryogenesis in cell suspensions of pigeonpea (Cajanus cajan L.) Plant Cell Tiss Org Cul xx 1-6

Rangasamy NS (1986) Somatic embryogenesis in angiosperm cell,tissue and organ cultures Proc Ind Acad Sci 247-271

Rao A, Srinivasan K, Rao KT (1973) The effect of Mandukaparni (*Centella asiatica*) on the gradual mental ability (Madhya) of mentally retarded children. Jour Res Edn Ind Med 8(4): 9-15

Rao Mohandas, K. G., Rao, M. S., Karanth, S. and Rao, G. .M. 1999. Effect of *Centella asiatica*) extract on rat CNS-A functional and morphological correlation. Indian Journal of Pharmacology, 31(1): 56.

Rao, A., Srinivasan, K. and Rao, K. T. 1973. The effect of Mandukaparani (*Centella asiatica*) on the general mental ability (Medhya) of mentally retarded children. Journal Res. Ind. Med., 8(4) : 9 - 15.

Rao, G., Vishnu, H. G., Shivakumar, K. and Parthiasarathi, G. 1996. Influence of aqueous extract of *Centella asiatica* (Brahmi) on experimental wounds in albino rats. Indian Journal of Pharmacology, 28(4) : 249 - 253.

Rao, P. S. 1965. *In vitro* induction of embryonal proliferation in *Santalum album* L. Phytomorphology, 15 : 175 - 179.

Rao, P. S., Suprasanna, P. and Ganapathi, T. 1996. Plant biotechnology and agriculture: prospects for crop improvement and increasing productivity. Science and Culture, 62(7-8) : 185 - 191.

Rao, U. P., Brahmam, M. and Saxena, H. O. 1985. Phytochemical survey of Mayurbhanj, Ganjam and Puri districts, (Orissa) for tannins, saponins, flavonoids and alkaloids. Indian drugs, 22 : 502 - 507.

Reddy, P. S., Gopal, G. R. and Lakshmi Sita, G. 1998. *In vitro* multiplication of *Gymnema sylvestre* R. Br.- An important medicinal plant. Curr. Sci., 75 : 843 - 845.

Reddy, R. V. 1995. Ethnobotanical and phytochemical studies on medicinal plant resources of Cuddapah district, A.P.India.Ph.D. Thesis, S.K.University, Anatapur, India.

Reinert, J. 1958. Morphogenese und ihre kontrollean gewebekulturen aus korotten Naturwssissens chaften. Planta 45: 344-346.

Reinhard E. (1974) Biotransformation of steroids via cell culture, In : Tissue culture and plant science , (Ed.) H.E. Street Academic press, New York, pp 433-459

Reinhard, E. (1974). Biotransformation of steroids via cell culture, In: Tissue Culture and Plant Science, (Ed.) H.E.Street, Academic Press, New York, pp.433-459.

Rout G.R., Saxena C., Samantaray S and Das P. (1999). Rapid plant regeneration from callus cultures of *Plumbago zeylanica* Plant Cell Tissue and Organ Culture 56: 47-51.

Roy A, Mukherjee AK and Rao CV (1975) Graded-hydrolysis studies on bael (Aegle marmelos (L.) Corr.) gum Carbohydrates Res 41: 219-226

Roy, A., Mukherjee, A.K. and Rao, C.V. (1975). Graded-hydrolysis studies on bael [*Aegle marmelos* (L.) Corr.] gum. Carbohydrates Res., 41: 219-226.

Roy, S. K., Islam, M. S. and Hadiuzzaman, S. 1998. Micropropagation of *Elaeocarpus robustus* Roxb. Plant Cell Rep., 17 : 810 - 813.

Roy, S. K., Islam, M. S., Sen, J. and Hadiuzzaman, S. 1993. Propagation of flood tolerant jackfruit (*Artocarpus heterophyllus*) by *in vitro* culture. Acta Hortic., 336 : 273 - 276.

Sabins, S.D. and Daniel, M. 1990. A phytochemical approach to economic botany, Ludhiana, India.

Sabita, B. and Sanghamitra, B. 1997. Rapid multiplication of *Jasminum officinale* L. by *in vitro* culture of nodal explants. Plant Cell Tiss. Org. Cult., 51 : 57 - 60.

Saha, T, Ghosh M and Sen S.K. (1999). Plant regeneration from cotyledonary explants of jute, *Corchorus capsularis* L. Plant Cell Rep. 18: 544-548.

Sahoo Y, Chand PK (1998) Factors influence of micropropagation of *Tridax procumbens*. Phytomorphology 48(2): 195-205

Sahoo Y, Pattnaik SK, Chand PK (1997) *In vitro* clonal propagation of an aromatic medicinal herb *Ocimum basilicum* L. (Sweet basil) by axillary shoot proliferation. *In Vitro* Cell Dev Biol Plant 33: 293-296

Sahoo, Y. and Chand, P. K. 1998a. *In vitro* multiplication of a medicinal herb, *Tridax procumbens* L. (Mexican daisy, coat buttons): Influence of explanting season, growth regulator synergy, culture passage and planting substrate. Phytomorphology, 48(2) : 195 - 205.

Sahoo, Y. and Chand, P. K. 1998b. Micropropagation of *Vitex negundo* L., a woody aromatic medicinal shrub, through high-frequency axillary shoot proliferation. Plant Cell Rep., 18 : 301 - 307.

Sanyal, M., Dutta Gupta, S., Jana, M. K. and Kundu, S. C. 1998. Shoot organogenesis and plantlet regeneration from leaf callus cultures of tuberose (*Polianthes tuberosa* L.). Plant Tissue Cult. Biotechnol., 4: 81 - 86.

Sarkar, P., Sinha Babu, S. P. and Sukul, N. C. 1998. Antifilarial effect of a combination of botanials from *Acacia auriculiformis* and *Centella asiatica* Pharmaceutical Biology, 36(2) : 107 - 110.

Sarker, R. H., Islam, M. R. and Hoque, M. I. 1997. *In vitro* propagation of Neem (*Azadirchia indica* A. Juss) plants from seedling explants. Plant Tiss. Cult., 7 : 125 - 133.

Saunders, J.W. and Tsai, C.J. 1999. Production of somatic embryos and shoots from sugarbeet callus: Effects of abscisic acid, other growth regulators, nitrogen source, sucrose concenteration and genotype. *In vitro* Cell Dev. Biol. 35: 18-24.

Saxena, A. P. and Vyas, K. M. 1981. Ethnobotanical records on infectious diseases from tribals of Banda district. J.Econ. Tax. Bot.,(Ludhiana),India.

Saxena, C., Palai, S. K., Samantaray, S., Rout, G. R. and Das, P. 1997. Plantlet regeneration from callus cultures of *Psoralea cordlifolia* L. Plant Growth Reg., 22 : 13 - 17.

Sen J, Sharma AK (1991) Micropropagation of *Withania somnifera* from germinating seeds and shoot tips. Plant Cell Tiss Org Cult 26: 71-73

Shah, R. R. and Dalal, K. C. 1980. *In vitro* multiplication of Glycyrrhiza. Curr. Sci., 49 : 69 - 71.

Shajahan A (1994) In vitro culture studies in mulberry genotype PhD thesis Bharathidasan University, Tiruchirappalli. Soth India.

Shanker, S. and Mohan Ram, H. Y. 1990. *In vitro* plantlet regeneration in the leguminous tree, *Sesbania sesban*. Phytomorphology, 40 : 43 - 52.

Sharma A, Jaiwal AN, Kumar S, Chaturvedi S, Tewari PV (1985) Role of brahmi (*Centella asiatica*) in educable mentally retarded children. Jour Res Edn Ind Med 4(1-2): 55-57

Sharma, A., Jaiswal, A. N., Kumar, S., Chaturvedi, S. and Tewari, P. V. 1985. Role of brahmi (*Centella asiatica*) in educable mentally retarded children. J. Research Education Indian Medicine, 4(1-2) : 55 - 57.

Sharma, V. and Padhya, M. A. 1996. *In vitro* rapid multiplication and propagation of *Crataeva nurvatla*. Indian J. Exptl. Biol., 34 : 243 - 246.

Sharp, W.R. Sandahl, M.R. Caldas, L.S. and Maraffa, S.B. (1980). The physiology of *in vitro* asexual embryogenesis. Hort. Rev. 2: 268-310.

Shetty, K. and Asano, Y. 1991. The influence of organic nitrogen sucrose on the induction of embryogenic callus in *Agrostis alba* L. J. Plant Physiol. 139: 82-85.

Shrivastava N and Rajani M. (1999). Multiple shoot regeneration and tissue culture studies on *Bacopa monnieri* (L.) Pennell. Plant Cell Rep. 18: 919-923.

Shukla SP, Mishra BK (1981) The psychotropic effect of medhyarasayana drug mandukaparni (*Hydrocotyle asiatica)* an experimental study- Part II. Jour Res Ayur Siddha 2(1): 1-10

Simard, M. H. 1985. Methodologies de selection de plants de fenouil amer (*Foeniculum vulgare*) tolerants av Phomopsis foeniculi et a ses prinicpes toxiques. Rapport de stage Ecole Nationale superienre d Horticulture, Versailles. Fr

Singh RP, Singh BD, Jaiswal HK , Singh RM, Singh RB, (1982) Organogenesis and callus culture of chickpea. Indian J. Agri Sci 52 : 86-90

Singh, R. H., Shukla, S. P. and Mishra, B. K. 1981. The psychotropic effect of medhyarasayana drug mandukaparni (*Hydrocotyle asiatica*) an experimental study - Part -II. Jour. Res. Ayur. Siddha, 2(1) : 1 - 10.

Singh, R.H. 2000. Rasayana theraphy: Evidence based relevance to aging, immunity and mental health. Proceedings of international congress on "Ayurveda-2000", 63 : 28 - 30.

Sir Edward Bailey, E. R. S. 1945. News and views. Nature, 155: 601.

Sivakumar G and Krishnamurthy K.V. (2000). Micropropagation of *Gloriosa superba* L. - an endangered species of Asia and Africa. Curr. Sci. 78(1): 30-32.

Skoog, F. and Miller, C. O. 1957. Chemical regulation of growth and organ formation in plant tissue culture *In vitro.* Symp. Soc. Exp. Biol., 11 : 118 - 131.

Smith MK and Drew (1990) current application of tissue culture in plant propagation and improvement . Australian J Plant Physiol 17 : 267-286

Solet, J. M., Bister-Miel, F., Galons, H., Spagnoli, R., Guignard, J. L. and Cosson, L. 1993. Glycosylation of thiocolchicine by a cell suspension culture of *Centella asiatica*. Phytochemistry, 33(4) : 817 - 820.

Srivastava, R., Shukla, Y.N. Sushil Kumar, 1997. Chemistry and pharmacology of *Centella asiatica*. A review. Journal of Medicinal and Aromatic Plant Sciences, 19(4) : 1049 - 1056.

Stephan, R. and Jayabalan, N. 2001. Propagation of *Coriandrum sitivum* L. through somatic embryogenesis. Indian J Exp. Biol., 39: 387 - 389.

Steward, F. C., Mapes, M. O. and Mears, K. 1985a. Growth and organized development of cultured cells. II. Organizaion in cultured growth from freely suspended cells. Am. J. Bot., 45 : 705-708.

Steward, F. C., Mapes, M. O. and Smith, J. 1985b. Growth and organized development of cultured cells. I. Growth and division of freely suspended cells. Am. J. Bot., 45 : 693 - 703.

Stohs SJ (1977) Biotransformation of steroids and cardiac glycosides through plant cell cultures , In : Plant tissue culture and its biotechnological application (Eds.) W.Barz, E. Reinhard and Rosenberg H. Lloydia 38 : 181-194

Stohs, S.J. (1977). Biotransformation of steroids and cardiac glycosides through plant cell cultures, In: Plant Tissue Culture and its Biotechnological Application (Eds.) W.Barz, E.Reinhard and Rosenberg, H. Lloydia., 38: 181-194.

Street HE (1977) Cell (suspension) culture-techniques In : H. E. Street (Eds.) Plant tissue and cell culture. Black well scientific publishers, Oxford, pp 11-30

Sudarsanam, G. 1987. Ethno- botanical survey and phyto-pharmaco-chemical screening of medicinal plants of chittoor district, Ph.D. Thesis, S.V.University, tirupati, India.

Sudha GC, Seeni S (1994) *In vitro* propagation and field establishment of *Adhatoda benddomei* CB Clarke a rare medicinal plant. Plant Cell Rep 13: 203-207.

Sudha, C. G. and Seeni, S. 1996). *In vitro* propagation of *Rauwolfia micrantha*, a rare medicinal plant. Plant Cell Tiss. Org. Cult., 44 : 243 - 248.

Suguna, L., Sivakumar, P. and Gowri Chandrakasan, 1996. Effects of *Centella asiatica* extract on dermal wound healing in rats. Indian Journal of Experimental Biology, 34 (12) : 1208 - 1211.

Tabata M, Hiraoka N , Ikenoue M Sano Y, and Konoshinea M (1978) Callus cultures and anthroquinone production in cassia tora Lloydia 38 : 131

Tabata, M., Hiraoka, N., Ikenoue, M., Sano, Y. and Konoshinea, M. (1978). Callus cultures and anthroquinone production in *Cassia tora*. Lloydia., 38: 131.

Tanira, M. M., Bashir, A. K., Dib, R., Goodwin, C. S., Wasfi, I. A. and Banna, N. R. 1994. Antimicrobial and phytochemical screening of medicinal plants of the United Arab Emirates. J. Ethnopharm., 41: 201 - 205.

Thomas, E. and Street, H. E. 1970. Organogenesis in cell suspension cultures of *Atropa bellodanna* L & A. Atropa cultivan lutean Doll Ann. Bot., 34 : 657 - 669.

Thomas, K. A., Martin, K. P. and Hariharan, M. 1996. *In vitro* Clonal multiplication of *Alpinia calcarata* Rosc. Phytomorphology, 46 : 133 - 138.

Thrope, T.A., Harry, I.S. and Kumar, P. P. 1991. Application of micropropagation to forestry. In: Micropropagation technology and appliation. Debergh & Zimmerman, R. H. (Eds.), Kluwer Academic Publ., Dordrecht. Pp 311 - 336.

Tideman, J. and Hawker, J. S. 1982. *In vitro* propagation of latex producing plants. Ann. Bot., 49 : 272 - 279.

Tiwari, V, Deo Singh B. and Nath Tiwari K. (1998). Shoot regeneration and somatic embryogenesis from different explants of Brahmi [*Bacopa monniera* (L.) Wettst.]. Plant Cell Rep. 17: 538-543.

Toth, K. F. and Lacy, M. L. 1992. Micropropagation of celary (*Apium graveolens* var. dulce) In: Bajaj, Y. P. S. (ed) Biotechnology in Agriculture and Forestry. V 19: Pp 218 - 230. Springer-Verlag Berlin, Heidelberg.

Tripathi, A. K., Jain, D. C., Sushil, K. and Kumar, K. 1996. Secondary metabolites and their biological and medicinal activities of piper species plants. J. Med. Arom. Plant. Sci., 2 : 302 - 321.

Trolinder, N. L. and Shang, X. 1991. *In vitro* selection and regeneration of cotton resistant to high temperature stress. Plant Cell Rep., 10 : 448 - 452.

Van Overbeek, J. (1942). Hormonal control of embryo and seedling cold spring Habor symposia on quantitative biology. 10: 126-134.

Vandemoortele, J. L., Billard, J. P. Bougard J and Gaspar, Th.1996. Micropropagation of parsley through axillary shoot proliferation. Plant Cell Tiss. Org. Cult., 44 : 25 - 30.

Vaquero F, Robles C and Ruiz ML (1993) A method for long-term micropropagation of Phaseolus coccineus . Plant Cell Rep 12 : 395-398

Vasil, V. and Vasil, I. K. 1986. Plant regeneration from friable embryogenic callus and suspension of *zea mays* L. J. Plant Physiol., 124 : 399 - 408.

Venkatachalam, P., Geetha, N. and Jayabalan, N. 1998. Influence of growth regulators on plant regeneration from epicotyl and hypocotyls cultures of two groundnut (*Arachis hypogea* L.) cultivars. J. Plant Biol., 41(1) : 1 - 8.

Vincent KA, Mathew KM, Hariharan M (1992) Micropropagation of *Kaempferia galanga* L. a medicinal Plant. Plant Cell Tiss Org Cult 28: 229-230

Vishwanath, M. P. and Jayanthi, M. 1997. Micropropagation of two species of *Rauvolfia* (Apocynaceae). Curr. Sci., 72(12) : 961 - 965.

Wakhlu, A. K. and Sharma, A. K. 1998. Somatic embryogenesis and plant regeneration in *Heracleum candicans* Wall. Plant Cell Rep., 17 : 866 - 869.

Wang, H. and Pierre, D. 1995. Somatic embrygenesis and plant regeneration in garden leek. Plant Cell, Tiss. Org. Cult., 43 : 21 - 28.

Wann, S. R. 1988. Somatic embryogenesis in woody species. Hort. Rev., 10 : 153 - 177.

Wayne, A. M., Jimmy, L. T. and Gary, A. T. 1995. Micropropagation of Mexican red bud ,*Cercis Canadensis* var. *mexicana* .Plant Cell Tiss. Org. Cult., 43 : 295 - 299.

Weatherhead, M. A., Burdon, T. and Henshaw, G. G. 1979. Effects of activated charcoal as an additive plant tissue culture media. Z. Pflanzenphysiol, 94 : 399 - 405.

Wilkins P and Dodds SH (1983) Tissue culture propagation of temperate fruit trees . In. Dodds JH (Eds) . Tissue culture of trees Connicticut, Avi Publications pp .133-136

Williams BL and Goodwin TW (1965) The Terpenoids of tissue cultures of Paul's scarlet rose Phytochemistry 4 : 81-88

Williams, B.L. and Goodwin, T.W. 91965). The terpenoids of tissue cultures of Paul's scarlet rose. Phytochemistry, 4: 81-88.

Winton LL (1978) Morphogenesis in clonal propagation of woody plants In : Frontiers of plant tissueculture Proc . 4 th International Congress of Plant Tissue Culture pp 419-426

Withers LA, and Street HE (1977) Development of plant cell cultures on production of phytochemical compounds, In : Plant tissue culture and its biotechnological application (Eds.) W. Barz, E.Reinhard and Zenk M.H., Springer - Verlag, Berlin and New york pp 226-244

Withers LA (1978) Plant cell cultures and sign of development on commercial scale,

Withers LA (1989) *In vitro* conservation and germplasm utilization In : Brown A.H.D , Frankel O.H., Marshall D.R., and Williamns J.T. (Eds.) The use of plant gemetic resources Cambridge, Cambridge University Press, pp 309-334

Withers, L.A. (1978). Plant cell cultures and sign of development on commercial scale, In: Frontiers of Plant Tissue Culture, (Ed.) T.A.Thorpe, The Bookstore, University of Calgary, Alberta, Canada, pp. 297-306.

Withers, L.A. and Stree, H.E. (1977). Development of plant cell cultures on production of phytochemical compounds, In: Plant Tissue Culture and Its Biotechnological Application, (Eds.) W.Barz, E.Reinhard and Zenk, M.H. Springer-Verlag, Berlin and New York, pp. 226-244.

Wong, K. C. and Tan, G. L. 1994. Essential oil of *Centella asiatica* (L.) Urban. Journal of Essential oil Research, 6(3) : 307 - 309.

Xin, S. Y. and Zhang, Z. Z. 1987. Explant tissue culture and platelet regeneration of sweet potato. Int. Acta. Botanica. Sinica., 23 : 114 - 116.

Yadav, R. C., Mohamed, T. S. and Grumet, R. 1996. High frequency shoot regeneration from leaf explants of muskmelon. Plant Cell Tiss. Org. Cult., 45: 207 - 214.

Yeoman and Mcleod 1977 Plant cell and tissue culture.S.Narayanaswamy Tata McGraw hill publishing company Ltd. New Delhi p 51.

Yeoman, 1987. Plant cell and tissue culture. Tata McGraw Hill publishing company Ltd. New Delhi, Pp 629-630.

Yoosook, C., Bunyapraphatsara, N., Boonyakiat, Y. and Kantasuk, C. 1999. Anti-herpes simplex virus activities of crude water extracts of thai medicinal plants. Phytomedicine, 6(6): 411-419.

You,R.L.,Wang,J.F.,Sung , Z.R.(1993).Impact of temperature on callus growth and somatic embryogenesis in carrot haploid cell line HA and its,temperature sensitive mutant lines. Chinese Journal of Botany 5(2):114-121.

Yu K., Christie BR and Pauls KD (1990) Effects of *Verticillium alboartrum* culture filtrate on somatic embryogenesis in alfalafa. Plant Cell Rep 8 : 509- 511

Zagorska N, Dimitrov B(1995). Induced androgenesis in alfalfa (*Medicago sativa L.*) Plant Cell Rep. 14: 249-252.

Zenk MH (1978) production of anthroquinone glycosides by cell cultures of *Morinda citrifolia* In : frontiers of plant tissue culture (Ed.) T.A. Thorpe IAPTC, Calgary , Canada pp 11.

Zenk MH, E I-Shagi H, Arens H, Stockgt J Weiler EW and Dew B (1977) In : plant tissue culture-Biotechnological application (Eds.) W.Barz, E.Reinhard and M.H. Zenk, Springer -Verlag, Berlin Newyork, pp27,37

Zenk, M.H. (1978). Production of anthroquinone glycosides by cell cultures of *Morinda citrifolia*, In: Frontiers of plant tissue cultures (Ed.) T.A.Thorpe. IAPTC, Calgary, Canada, pp.11.

Zenk, M.H. E I-Shagi, H., Arens, H., Stckgt,J., Weiler, E.W. and Dew, B. (1977). In: Plant Tissue Culture-Biotechnological application (Eds.) W.Barz, E.Reinhard and M.H.Zenk, Springr-Verlag, Berlin, New York, pp.27-37.

Zhang Shi-Yu and Cheng Kuo-Chang 1989. I Angelica sinensis (Oliv) Diels.: *In vitro* culture, regeneration and the production of medicinal compounds. In: bajaj YPS (ed) Biotechnology in Agriculture and Forestry, Vol 7 (pp 1-22). Springer-Verlag, berlin, Heidelberg.

Zhong Z, Smith HG & Thomas HT. (1993). Micropropagation of wild beet (*Beta maritime*) from inflorescence pieces Plant Growth Regulation 12: 53-57.

Zimmerman JL (1993). Somatic embryogenesis - A model for early development in higher plants. The Plant Cell 5: 1411-1423.

www.ingramcontent.com/pod-product-compliance
Lightning Source LLC
Chambersburg PA
CBHW080216170726
48282CB00030B/1140
* 9 7 8 8 1 9 4 6 5 0 0 7 2 *